the Mediator

the Mediator

his Strategy for Power

Richard Grey Swartzbaugh, Ph.D.

Howard Allen
Box 76
Cape Canaveral, Florida 32920

First Printing

Library of Congress Catalog Card No. 72–94968
Copyright © 1973 by Richard Grey Swartzbaugh
Printed in the United States of America

Contents

Foreword

In my efforts to comprehend my experiences as an American, I discovered Richard Swartzbaugh in an obscure Scottish anthropology journal. He wrote lucidly about the relations of people to one another, to their possessions, and to the land. We corresponded at length over a period of three years on many subjects. Dr. Swartzbaugh has invited me to write this Foreword because, as he generously claims, the book largely has grown out of our correspondence.

Although my area of specialization in the physical sciences is remote from anthropology, I recognized that Dr. Swartzbaugh and I have common interests and concerns. My childhood background in a blue-collar neighborhood in Philadelphia and my present career in applied mathematics has allowed me to experience America at various levels. These levels should have certain psychological and cultural characteristics in common. For that matter, the need for such continuity is generally felt among people of the working and middle classes, among urban and rural Americans, and among Northerners and Southerners. The meeting ground, it would seem, is a new kind of populism—a viewpoint given vigorous expression in this book.

Living among different classes and ethnic groups teaches one to be tactful and diplomatic. But in America diplomacy has become a substitute for a continuity of society. Families with a long history in the country move around even faster than recent arrivals. Few true communities are formed. The process has been encouraged by a Government all too aware that *a rootless mob is far easier to manipulate than people attached to some place they call home!*

Ambitious Americans have considered the people and land little more than an expendable resource in their quest for wealth and power. Keeping the country together has required unprecedented economic largess, mixed with coercion and delivered in small amounts at critical times. But every day this formula works a little less.

If and when America relinquishes its role as a world power, as it now appears to be doing, the disoriented majority may have a chance to experience a nationhood more meaningful than the empty legalism of citizenship. Something of the old America will remain; but something new will have to be added.

This book is written by an American and principally for Americans. There is more than a little danger that it will go unheeded here and be taken up elsewhere. Nevertheless it has been a special privilege to see this book through its formative stages, as you, the reader, will soon realize.

FOSTER MORRISON

Rockville, Maryland
December, 1972

I

THE STATE AS MAXIMUM MEDIATION

Social engineering: the science of playing one faction against the other and stepping in the middle as mediator. This is a dangerous game. In being *between* factions the mediator cannot be *of* them. His power depends, paradoxically, on the fact that he is an outsider, even an outcast. Conversely, an outsider, one shunned by his own society, has the best chance to rise to prestige and influence by interposing himself between parties who are mutually suspicious but who desire some kind of contractual accord. The paradox of the mediator is that his greatest success and splendor are also his worst peril. In reconciling groups on the level of practical diplomacy, he makes himself, in relation to the deepest cultural values of peoples, the enemy of the very groups he serves.

In large pluralistic societies the role of mediator has been largely taken by the state. Where diverse and mutually hostile populations come together, the state appears between them as a compensation for a lack of trust. Intervening to facilitate some co-operative enterprise, the state may be thought of as a kind of *contract* expressed as bureaucracy. But like the individual arbiter in smaller communities, the state must frequently take on the attributes and symbols of an outsider to society. It is important to note here that it is not generally the ruler, unless he is also a holy man, but the priest or shaman who is a go-between in the pure sense of the word. The priest works through esoteric and "universal" symbols rather than through direct personal coercion. These very symbols to some degree isolate the priest from personal associations. Therefore the state itself, as a universal and abstract and "esoteric" structure, must progressively distance and alienate itself from participation in any particular group. It becomes insular and oblivious to the tide of emotional and instinctual life in the relations of its citizens as they jostle one another in direct contacts.

These contacts are always changing. The state is in danger in that it can never absolutely stabilize the relations between its constituent groups. Either they close together, rendering the mediative function of the state unnecessary. Or they finally part ways entirely.

In rising above a personal and organic basis of power, the state must finally shift to an entirely new strategy for dominance, namely, an abstract strategy. Once this stage of aloofness is reached, far from seeking direct involvements with actual people, the state becomes suspicious and hostile regarding personal ties, not only between itself and its citizens but among the citizens themselves. The state well understands that when even two people meet on the level of primal instincts, *a tiny but significant conspiracy is hatched*—not simply against the state as a particular form of political life, but against the entire abstract, contractual principle of human group life of which the state is the ultimate expression! Between the state and its citizens is bureaucracy. Between man and man are principles which are not hierarchical as such but which stabilize structures between state and citizen: law, commerce, religion and the ideology of human brotherhood.

The Berlin philosopher Kaspar Schmidt, writing under the nom de plume Max Stirner, asserted: "The state cannot tolerate that man stands to man in a direct relationship: it must step between them as *mediator*, must *intervene*. What Christ was, what the holy men and the Church have been, the state has become, namely, 'mediator.' It tears man from man in order to interpose itself as abstractions in the middle." [1]

Where such a bureaucracy does not finally suffer a direct revolution it finally dissolves in the abstract impersonalness that it would force upon its subjects. The Ottoman Turks, striving to hold together a complex situation of pluralism, lost their racial and ethnic continuity altogether and became—a bureaucracy! H. G. Wells describes the late Ottoman power structure as ". . . an army of clerks, scribes, writers, and accountants [which] swarmed into . . . offices and gradually swept the whole power of the government into their own hands by separating the Commander of the Faithful from any direct intercourse with his subjects." [2] Unlike the Chinese Mandarin class, which for centuries interceded between ruler and subject, the Ottoman bureaucracy could not perpetuate itself.

First appearing as a small and cohesive population and as such conquering vast regions, the Ottomans sacrificed peoplehood and culture to an abstract system of power. Within this system they died out. The structure outwardly sanctioned by the Muslim world religion, rather than being bred and culturally imparted, was only recruited and indoctrinated. Toynbee says: "[Recruits] were obtained from various Infidel sources: from beyond the frontiers by capture in war, by purchase in the slave market. . . Discipline was severe and punishment savage, while on the other hand there was deliberate and unceasing appeal to ambition." [3] Even the royal family was in effect part of this "slave family," in that the sultan's mother was traditionally a harem slave. Family life was discouraged, what few children there were could not inherit property or position, and the public servants were always threatened with execution. What the system discouraged, essentially, were instincts. Substituted were such abstractions as hierarchy and religion. The Ottoman system thus became the thing it had tried to make its subjects—a rootless, raceless body of slaves.

Denying itself personal and organic continuity, the state cannot allow its subject populations a more basic solidarity. It therefore attempts to dissolve direct bonds within racial and ethnic groups by shuffling the groups together in forced contact, then structuring the uprooted and disoriented individuals by abstract arbitration. Integration of black and white children in American schools, for example, has behind it the same thought Charlemagne had when he dispersed the Saxons because he could not destroy their unity. The Maoists have shifted large numbers of the Han ethnic group to Mongolia, while bringing many Mongolians south.[4] The Russians have transported and shuffled up Ukrainians and Poles. While Russian bureaucrats have now and then given publicity to folk customs of various regions of their empire—it is more a suspicious preoccupation than a real enthusiasm—they have proven themselves in the long run hostile to self-contained corporate cultures.

Now America, not only as a state but as a nexus of commerce and technology, has in the past decades come to represent primarily the mediative principle. The beginnings of true culture in the Colonies and the isolated pockets of culture still existing have been all but swamped by an "American system" which is called a culture but, since it has no historical or racial roots, is really the antithesis of culture—a cold abstraction. But America is still a new country. The abstract system has prevailed because Americans, who are still essentially strangers to one another, have not yet found a real cultural and national mode of relationship. Inhabited as it is by disparate ethnic groups and individuals, America has bridged the distance between its citizens with theories and theoretical social structures. The confusion and unhappiness have come as people depending on the system have tried to justify it as the permanent order of things.

The mediated society is an "integrated" society. Integration demands the elimination of personal and instinctual ties of men and women of the same limited regional and racial groups. These organic and historical bonds of empathy and trust are suppressed in favor of formal contractual ties. Artistic expressions of discrete cultures, tribes and races are suppressed in favor of systemization in abstract structures. The entire instinctual and archetypal and moral principal of cohesion is cut into and disrupted, leaving a drifting residue of isolated egos who can reorient themselves only by adhering to these structures.

The concern of this book, specifically, is social mediation. In America's newly integrated schools the young children are often required to engage in what is called informal classroom discussion but is in reality a gossip session for the purpose of bringing out into the open the most intimate details of the children's private family life. The program's sponsors, the directors of the gossip, profess that this intimate talk will make the children, black and white, realize that they are "all alike" and "all human beings" in that they have a common everyday family life! But they do not have anything like a common social life! The purpose of this group self-revelation can better be understood by relating it to a wide range of contemporary school subjects such as civics and "sex education." These courses all have the function of "integrative" mediation.

But before social integration is possible, the private and exclusive—and exclusivist—domain of the family must be opened through the enlightenment or illumination of inward feelings and drives. Individual meanings and motives are summoned before the abstract collectivity, the self-conscious supergroup where they are subjected to the "criticism" of abstract reason. The basic terms of this rationality are precisely the terms of the supergroup's mode of structure and cohesion. The abstract analysis of feeling and instinct, like any analysis, logically entails an

5

abstract synthesis in the other direction which can also be the basis of an artificial mode of human cohesion. This proposition is the essential idea behind the Social Contract theory, an early formulation of the premise of most modern sociological theory. According to the Social Contract ideology, reason and abstract thought are the underlying foundation of the Contract.

Inward organic values are therefore drawn out by the mediator where they can be looked at by every stranger. In the process of group examination they assume a different aspect and even look ridiculous, thereby dissolving as self-evident truths. The individual wishing to avoid total rootlessness is now prone to take his truths from the abstract collectivity. "Confession" has long been effectively used by the Chinese to break up threatening solidarity in prisoner-of-war camps and peasant communes. The group or community dissolves as an organic unit as the men talk personally about one another and themselves in front of the group as a whole. In the Korean War many American soldiers subjected to this confession simply isolated themselves and died. What is confessed here are exclusivist bonds and privately shared meanings. For these emotional ties the mediator substitutes his own symbols through which the people must submissively mediate relationships if they are to have contacts on any terms. The director of mediation is in full charge in that he can manipulate the abstract symbols or terms of the "contract." The mediator "clears" all relations in the system, which is under his control.

For the instinctually cohesive family, clan and tribe, which are the containers of history and culture, is substituted an "integrated" but organically dissolved sociological subsystem. While public suspicion has been commonly directed toward grandiose, fantastic strategies for the integration of whole races, the more subtle ideas implicit in the most innocuous-appearing sociology courses called "the family" have been overlooked. The ultimate goal of social engineering in family "integration" is the mediation of relationships within the most elemental human grouping. Family members united through integration are divided personally. The organically cohesive family is broken down and replaced by the sociological abstraction of a "primary group," where, if the reality is brought to approximate the model, even the mother is attached to her child by virtue of a so-called social role, a conditioned sense of duty which amounts to a kind of legalistic "contract" with the child. The possibility that even the family could be subjected to social engineering derives, perhaps, from the principal theoretician of the Social Contract.

Rousseau put it this way: "The oldest of societies, and the only society that is in any sense natural, is the family. Yet we must not overlook the role of agreements even here: the children do not remain tied to the father beyond the period during which they have need of him in order to preserve themselves. . . If they continue together, they no longer do so out of natural necessity but rather out of choice, so that thenceforth even the family keeps itself alive only by agreement." [5] Once the abstract social principle has penetrated the family, the last instinctual bond is dissolved. Mediation is the last resort.

Although Rousseau is popularly conceived as the "back-to-nature" philosopher, he seems on the subtle point of the family to have held the social viewpoint of a mediator. For that matter, the positive and affirmative connection between the state and its "adversary," the primitivist and ascetic, has not been fully understood. As one who withdraws from "existing society" the recluse is in the outside position to create new symbols which mediate new relationships. The ascetic is a prophet. The paradox of primitivism and "nature love" in combination with a highly rationalistic and contractual view of society is resolved by the following consideration: it is precisely a withdrawal from so-called existing society—either an individual or mass re-

7

treat—which renders an individual prophet or an entire mass (today, the hippies; earlier the Buddhists and the European Youth Movement) sensitive to, and disposed to embrace, new symbols of mediation. Hence the recluse and ascetic Saint Francis, who distinguished himself for his simple love of all living creatures, was, at least latently, a social rationalist. As evidence of this there is the amusing but highly significant anecdote related by Kenneth Clark in *Civilization:* "St. Francis. . . persuades a fierce wolf that terrified the people of Gubbio to make a pact by which, in return for regular meals, he will leave the citizens alone. 'Give me your paw,' said St. Francis, and the wolf gave his paw." It is the paradox of several other important ascetics and saints, among them St. Benedict, that they finally involve themselves politically as arbiters.

Social self-isolation, and in the asceticism of withdrawal the generation of fresh symbolism of mediation, is, as I say, the role of the prophet. The prophet is the one who goes into the wilderness and is prone to trances and visions. On the other hand, the priesthoods which spring up in the name of a prophet and his vision are highly abstract associations which integrate themselves into established state hierarchies. At the same time the priesthoods retain the original symbolism of outsideness. But as an established power the priests are extremely alert and defensive concerning the possible appearance of a new prophet who will upset their order.

The emphasis of this book is not on the prophet but on the priest—in other words, on the pure symbolism of outsideness. The priest's claim to power by virtue of this symbolism can best be understood by comparing the priest to the lawyer. A legal contract is an abstract structural safeguard or stabilizer where the contracting parties do not entirely trust one another. In this respect the contract is a negative compensation. Where the distrust is the greatest —and this is why the greatest legal systems have come out of political contexts such as that of ancient Rome—the symbolism of contractual trust is the greatest. Suppose, then, that every human relationship were in the formal terms of a legal contract. *What would this mean for the status and number of lawyers?*

Of course the men who understand one another least are men of different ethnic, religious, historical, national and racial backgrounds. The social mediator, who, as I will show, can exist as an outsider only by reconciling and stabilizing relationships between distrustful individuals and groups, is quite satisfied with the stiff formality of a contractual social relationship. In our own day he is even proud of the "confrontation" diplomacy, "dialogue," "encounter," "sensitivity training" and all the strained pomp of "reconciliation" in American race relations.

Yet he wants to go further. The contractual structure of racial and national diplomacy is not in itself a goal but merely a stage along the way to the point where *all* human relationships, within the races as well as between them, and even within the family, are legalistic. If this transpired, men could not have bonds at all except through the formal terms of the mediator.

The conclusion is unavoidable that mediation must absorb and drain away the life energy which would otherwise be devoted to existence as such, that is, to a complete emotional and esthetic involvement with a world in which one feels he belongs. Mediation not only spans the gaps between separate spheres of concrete being but must translate them into an abstraction. Structures which are not cultures may be integrative and lump vast masses of people in giant systems. But they are not existentially relevant. Human life, in the language of Existentialism, no longer has *being*. "Integrated" life is rather a condition of *being-between*, being, namely, in the "land of the mediator."

There is a further consideration: it is characteristic of a system of mediation that it *inverts* the values of self-contained and limited regional cultures, turning them on

9

their heads, *"sie auf den Kopf stellen,"* as Nietzsche said. The aspiration of culture, as of any living organism, is *form*. The values of the outsider who is the only "universal man" are, on the other hand, affirmative only of an existence in its highest generality. Great world mediative ideas are vaguely and sometimes precisely opposite of the values of regional cultures which depend upon definite boundaries and limitations for a frame of reference. With regard to limited organic situations, universalist ideas are in their final application thought to be, if not altogether unacceptable, then in some sense "impossible." This is not to say that these values are not taken seriously. On the contrary, *they are often held sacred*. The so-called impossible values are the ones which, with respect to their applicability to trans-organic, interracial and international contacts, are virtually holy. Similarly the mediators, symbolically and ritually defined as outsiders and even as rejects from personalistic society, are precisely the most revered priests.

The true state arises, as Ortega y Gasset perceived, not from any idea of natural frontiers, race or language but rather as "an invitation issued by one group of men to other human groups to carry out some enterprise in common." [6] For Ortega the state is mediation. "The State begins when groups naturally divided find themselves obliged to live in common. This obligation. . . implies an impelling purpose, a common task which is set before the dispersed groups. Before all, the State is a plan of action and a program of collaboration. . . [The] State-principle is the movement which tends to annihilate the social forms of internal existence, and to substitute for them a social form adequate to the new life, lived externally." [7]

But what is the source of these "purposes" and "tasks" for which men come together? They do not arise out of nothing any more than the responses and solutions to the tasks are automatic. The highest missions are conceived by a closely communicating elite—of artists, soldiers, statesmen—who understand one another by virtue of a common history, tradition and race. Where these historical and cultural goals are absent, where peoples and individuals are so diverse that they cannot have important tasks in common, they cannot effectively cooperate. The state, which cannot artificially invent tasks, is superfluous.

The "mission" presently imposed by the American superstate—the satiation of the imagined material needs of the great masses—is scarcely enough to generate enthusiasm among a vigorous creative elite. Rather this so-called purpose is the magical but purely pragmatic conjuration of the mediator in his attempt to justify the state and its stabilizing legal and financial modes of abstract relationship. It should be understood that the mediator himself is in no real sense creative. It is indeed a miracle of empty cleverness that he can exist with so little creativity. He merely links together centers of potential enterprise and, perhaps, suffocates them in the process. Yet the state exists not for citizens, not even for the impoverished citizens. It exists rather for the mediator!

II

THE MEDIATOR AS SOCIAL
PHILOSOPHER

An important theme of social philosophy has been the
idea that human social bonds, as opposed to the relations of
animals, are fundamentally abstract. The primary human
ties are said to be linguistic and, insofar as language has a
formal logical structure, "rational." Reason in its social
application is legalistic and contractual. The intellectual,
who has evolved from the priest of more primitive societies, has developed this social concept with a great deal
at stake. His ideas and esoteric symbols are more than as-
sertions about reality. *They are modes of human relationships.* The philosopher specializing in the manipulation of
symbols thus, inasmuch as he is also priest, scribe and
lawyer operating abstract and legalistic structures, has control of human relationships.

Plato believed that existing society was based on instincts
and organic impulses. Nevertheless his utopia would transcend instincts to approximate an ideal or abstraction "un-
corrupted" by any physical reality, even by sense experience. In *The Republic* Plato shrewdly proposed that
the organic continuity of tradition be broken by removing
parents from the cities and by entrusting the education of
children to philosopher kings whose spiritual nature already conformed to the heavenly realm of ideas. The rule
of the philosophical elite, unlike that of the regional aristo-

crat, was not to be personal but abstract. In disrupting historical continuity the inner instinctual cohesion of traditional society would be shattered, demanding the mediative intervention by the philosopher. The pure idea or Form, which in Platonic metaphysics is the source of all true ethical value, was the unifying principle of the utopia. Therefore as an abstract idea the new society alone of all societies would be self-justifying.

For Plato only the philosopher was capable of a total abstract orientation; he dismissed the trader and money-man as materialists corrupted by the interests of the flesh and the senses. He however overlooked that it is precisely the commercialists whose outlook is perhaps most consistently abstract. Money could have laid, and in Athens of that time was already beginning to lay, the groundwork for an abstract society—although hardly a utopia! Plato, however, was tied to the idea that the foundations must be laid by the traditional aristocracy.

It is more than a coincidence that Plato proposed an ahistorical and trans-regional society at the very time Athens, defeated and culturally exhausted, had run out of history and was no longer a region. The city was without a felt and emotional sense of continuity and morale. Solon's Laws, which were abstract political designations cutting through cohesive clans living in Athens, had started a process of abstract definitions which ended finally in an extension of citizenship to foreigners in Athens on grounds of the technicality of residence. Plato's pure abstraction or society of Forms, like Augustine's City of God vis-à-vis the Roman civilization which followed Greece, was the philosophical fulfillment of legalistic tendencies. Deprived of any orientation through instincts and ingrained custom, Plato's Athens was grasping at abstractions as the only source of unity and order.

Contemporary social scientists have vigorously promoted two viewpoints as favorable to the possibility of social engineering—*behaviorism* and *superorganicism*. The first position is that while instinctual factors are pertinent to social structure, they are absolutely conditionable and malleable. Instincts may be molded and stretched according to traditional values; but at least theoretically they could be brought to conform with intellectual and abstract values.

The second view is that the problem of instincts and even of human "psychology" is irrelevant to social structures, which derive entirely from intellectual structures. Whatever instincts man may have he is, as a social being, abstract and contractual. Language is a meta-biological communication system that is secondarily a social system. In both the behaviorist and superorganicist views *ideas* are the actual governing force. And it should be remembered that *by ideas, ideas can be changed.* The sociologist as philosopher king is simply the one who is *aware* that social relationships are abstract and who can therefore plan and integrate them in their total generality. This awareness is the sociologist's claim to rule. Even enemies in the ranks of intellectuals—Plato and the Sophists are some of history's more famous enemies—agreed that society, in being constituted through abstract mediating bonds, can and should be engineered by intellectual intervention.

Thomas Hobbes (1588–1677) sought the same order in human society that Newton had found in the objective universe. This was an order of the human mind that conformed to the Divine Mind. But social organization could not be attributed to instincts which, according to the contemporary picture of social life of lower animals, were thought blind and chaotic. Ordered and co-operative life was believed possible exclusively within human and "rational" society.

Before the advent of "true society" men had lived a life that was free but violent, impoverished and short, a *bellum omnium contra omnes.* Men in the original state had been unrestrained individualists who could pursue any objective or yield to any drive the moment it arose, so long as their efforts were not opposed by the superior force of other men. Natural individualism was believed to persist even into modern times as a central though subdued feature of human character. Freeing the personality from an imposed abstract order would release this self-assertion. But of course, depending on whether the underlying human character was regarded as antisocial and aggressive or merely passive, ideas varied regarding the extent to which it was necessary to regulate and suppress such a personality. Hobbes and Rousseau took opposite views. However they both regarded the individual on an instinctual and personal level as an essentially isolated asocial atom. A man becomes truly social only through reason and language. For the Social Contract thinkers not only was there no such thing as essential instinctual cohesion but, on the contrary, what instincts existed were regarded contrary to the whole moral purpose of man.

Since human intercourse was regarded as chaotic on an instinctual level, the Social Contract theorists believed it should be abstractly ordered. This organization from the outset of true human life was provided by language. Language was the basic diagnostic trait which set man apart from animals. Rationally structured communication finally crystallized as an external legalistic and contractual agreement. In learning to reason and to communicate rational ideas men could express and formalize their desired peaceful and co-operative life in the Social Contract. Or they could at any rate collectivize and organize aggression. The Social Contract *is* in effect society. Otto Gierke says: "If civil society in general was merely the result of a contractual act, whereby individual rights were pooled in order that individual objects might henceforth be socially pursued, such society must, in the last analysis, resolve itself into an aggregate of mere legal connections between individuals." [1]

Language brought with it the man of the word—originally a social philosopher, lawyer, trader, priest and bureaucrat all in the person of one man. His symbols of human brotherhood and unity, although they were in themselves anti-hierarchical, suggested to the ruler the horizontal unity of his kingdom. The chief therefore kept the intellectual by his side to reinforce his power. As the ruler rose above his people and his kingdom expanded to include more diverse groups, the priestly intellectual became an indispensable mediator between the leader and his subjects. For that matter it was much to the advantage of the ruler to adopt the esoteric strategy of the priest. Constantine was one of the most famous rulers to use religion to cement his realm.

In the viewpoint of the Social Contract thinkers the abstract and symbolic side of power is more decisive than the personal factor because in man rationality is dominant over instincts. As societies became more complex, and as the feature of pluralism became more prominent, the intellectual would have a greater share of the power—but only because in his view he represents what man is *ab origine!*

It followed from this view that real moral existence could be attributed only to the individual on the one hand, and to the superstate on the other. A secondary and derivative reality was ascribed to limited groups or divisions within the state, including those with a venerable basis in history and race. The medium-sized group had significance only as an aspect of the state. Therefore rather than being affirmed in themselves, personalistic regional groups could justifiably be abolished or, what is the same, be reduced to the artificial categories of the supersystem. But in order to achieve this type of group it was necessary also to isolate the individual theoretically—and to isolate him in practice from instinctual contacts. Gierke says: "True, the local community was treated as a stage on the road to the State; but in the State itself, when once it had come into existence, this community was only allowed the significance of a constituent part or division." [2]

Structuralism and social anthropology are the modern heirs of Social Contract theory. Structuralism, which shares the abstractionist bias of Social Contract philosophy, is equally radical. It asserts that the most archaic and primitive societies, and even the family, insofar as they are specifically human groups, are fundamentally abstract and mediated. Extended families are seen in theoretical terms as a nexus of *contractual* agreements or "kinship systems." All societies are considered as mediated from their very inception through *language*. The order and logic of society has its source in the inherent logic of language. Claude Lévi-Strauss gives Structuralism its most radical formulation: "Men communicate by means of symbols and signs; for anthropology everything is symbol and sign, when it acts as intermediary between two subjects." [3]

The conception of society as a nexus of mediating abstractions is an intellectualist assumption. It is an unquestioned dogma, and for good reason. As mediators the intellectuals—the priests and scribes—can sit at the throne of the monarch. They have been able to interpose themselves between ruler and subject, and between subject and subject. The social mediator's role is seen as a higher, more elegant and morally righteous refinement of the general mode of social intercourse—language.

The presumed need of common people for symbols to mediate in everyday practical affairs raises the possibility of a world bureaucracy run by an ethnically heterogeneous but ideologically uniform association of intellectuals. But if human relations were derived from fixed and genetically transmitted instincts, and if, despite wide extension through symbols, relations always had to finally come back to instincts, men would ultimately give priority to organic and "pre-logical" groupings. Instincts therefore challenge the priest's and intellectual's bid for universal authority. Programmed as he is, however, to mediate between broad groupings among which there are only weak biological ties, the intellectual generalizes about all human relationships.

Recently a group of scientists called ethologists have reported research concerning instincts, or to use their new and fancier term, "innate releasing mechanisms." Much of this work, which originated in Europe, has found its way to a general book club audience through the popular writings of Robert Ardrey and Konrad Lorenz. However, the academic behavioral sciences, as a branch of the mediation establishment, remain highly suspicious of the ethological viewpoint. The implications for ideology are only too apparent. In general the public seems inclined to accept the view that instincts exist, forcing certain concessions among the academicians. But the tempo of their resistance can be expected to sharpen. They have a great deal to lose. Their interests are not merely in the uniformity and credibility of a pure ideology but the belief in the feasibility of their own practical intervention, as extensions of state bureaucracy, in the actual social life of citizens.

Only intellectuals attempt to attain a perfect uniformity of ideology because they alone habitually depend on ideas for cohesion and structure *within their own ranks*. The masses, while they are relatively indifferent to new ideas, are, so long as they have traditional cultures and instinctual relations, seldom truly dogmatic. They do not depend upon abstractions. Common people listen politely and sometimes even with interest to the intellectuals. But inside the intellectual's establishment men are, instinctually speaking, outsiders in relation to one another. Here abstractions, pertaining as they do to human relationships and hierarchical structures, make a serious difference. Ideas are not simply representations of the nature of external reality but are a necessary mode of human relationship. Hence the danger of the heterodox thinker within the ranks who would not simply challenge old philosophical and scientific truths but would upset the order of intellectuals. Such stability in the intellectual order is also encouraged by political leaders who see such order extending to their worldly kingdoms. For this reason, says Wells, Constantine "made a great effort to reconcile these differences [at Nicaea in 325] in order to have one uniform and harmonious teaching in the community . . ." [3]

III

CONTRACTS VERSUS INSTINCTS: THE HUNTING BAND

The best mediator is the one who is an outsider with respect to "closed" and "instinctual" society. Lacking instinctual social relations he must orient himself according to abstractions. If abstractions are the definitive trait of man, the mediator is therefore the most human of all men. Man is the being who is always trying to "get outside himself," that is, beyond the narrow sphere of instincts and thereby "opening" himself to a world of definite physical objects. An object is a thing which is sought and (in the double sense of attained and understood) grasped by abstractions. The abstraction which differentiates man from animals is a *mediative* bond vis-à-vis the external world.

The thesis of this chapter is that man exists by "opening" himself to an abstract world of targets and thereby frees himself from instincts or any specifically biological or organic orientation. But lest he lose himself entirely in endless and unfamiliar vistas (he has been exploring them only for a brief million years), he must at some point return to the sphere of elemental instincts and "close" himself to the world.

The world of particular and distant targets, as opposed to social relations which are biologically timeless, does not evoke the instincts that enable man to grasp the world spontaneously and naturally. The contact must be abstract in the minimal sense of *visual*. Abstract thought seems at the present stage of psychological research to be derived from a sense of form or gestalt which is built into visual perception. The relationship with the visual object is nevertheless a psychically remote as well as a spatially remote relationship. The problem of the present discussion, however, is not the connection between the man and his objective or target but a man's relation with his fellow human being.

Of particular concern is a male human being's bond with other males in the context of the hunting band, the target- and objective-oriented association. Human life in its primordial essence may be regarded as carnivorous and "masculine." Feminine life in the base camp, with its emphasis on raising children and its simple and nonvisual attention to nearby food sources, is in the terms of this discussion merely "instinctual." In this sense the males, in setting up a separate hunting camp, "went against" or pulled away from primordial instincts.

In the mediated relationship men have something interposed between them. While human beings still have essential instincts of social cohesion they also have indirect ties mediated by an objective or object which is outside the sphere of instincts. Men first began having mediated relationships when they had to co-ordinate their efforts to pursue *targets*, the fleet game animals which were the original objectives. Male hunters who had to venture far from their base camps and families entered into a new kind of relationship which was not a felt bond but a pragmatic alliance. The new tie emphasized symbolism where it was weak in instinctual content, which, however, could be revitalized when the men returned to their families. In directing themselves toward an objective or target the men were temporarily estranged in their instinctual relationships. And insofar as they had to postpone returning to their base camp, the objective itself, and the contractual bond which defined their respective relationships toward the objective, became the new principle of cohesion. In principle, however, with or without the contract, the essential and primal mediator was the objective.

The objective is "beyond" the social group, in the distance. Man is a distance-oriented being. He has been a hunter for a million years, leaving the closed forests for open savannas. He entered a world of wide vistas and, in a psychic sense, pure space. He rapidly stood upright on strong legs, his arms free to carry weapons. But of essential importance was the fact that he could concentrate on a target in the distance and, finally, could think about the target even when it had disappeared from sight. It is significant that man, who did not descend from a long line of hunters (he is the only primate who hunts), moved slowly in comparison to, say, leopards and carnivorous birds. Doggedly pursuing game that ran in rapid spurts, he had to keep fixed in mind a representation of the game. The target became an abstract idea, in other words, an object in the transcendental sense. Other carnivores hunt only what they can see and smell. It was man's capacity to "visualize" what he could not actually see that transformed him from a pursuer of animals to a hunter in the wider sense, namely, an *economic* being.

Man as a carnivorous species looks at his world as a nexus of definite points connected by abstract lines. The eyes of a herbivore are on the side of its head, giving it a defensive and diffuse world-image. But the eyes of the carnivore bring particular things into sharp three-dimensional focus. Vision here is dense, directed and pointed. Two co-ordinated binocular eyes close around the particular object in preparation for the grasping by the hand. Finally the object is "grasped" by an *idea*, namely, as an object in the theoretical sense.

The world of the hunter is visual and abstract. But while in an important sense defining his humanity, the object is still beyond him, aloof and "distant" from him.

The nomadic hunter forever had to forsake what was nearby and familiar, and to uproot his family in order to pursue elusive game into some distant land. Man is unique in this respect. It is a fact of some interest that even so mobile a predator as the lion will not venture out of its familiar home territory even though its game has seasonally gone elsewhere. But man, and particularly the male human being, is indeed a wanderer, "the arrow longing for the other shore," in Nietzsche's excellent phrase.

The man had no specific instincts to pursue this or that animal or thing. He also did not have the natural strength or speed. When African forests shrank at the beginning of the Pleistocene he was forced not only out of his familiar home territory *but out of the "environment" (Umwelt) altogether and into a radically different existence, into a "world" (Welt)*. This new "world" was not, as it is for the herbivore, a chain or sequence of cues and stimuli but an *abstract map*.

Man's intellect mediated the transition. Intelligence is accentuated where the organism overcomes inertia. Even the flea is intelligent insofar as its motion needs sensuous directions. Man's *eyes* were most responsive to distant points and could most directly chart a course to them. It was his brain which could "see" to points beyond the horizon. The paradox is that this very "world" which defines man as man is still, even after his million years of stalking and conquering, remote, foreign, uncertain and fearsome!

This is not to say that a practical objective can never be "personalized" and incorporated into the vital and instinctual sphere of the man. He can extend his primal feelings and archetypal ideas, which are ultimately social in derivation and content, to the objective. It thereby becomes a part of this social life. The margin where the object intersects with social feelings is the realm of *art*, in which object-oriented enterprises must ultimately be anchored.

This personalization of hunting and technical effort is necessary for the morale and sense of mission of the pragmatic alliance, the feeling of the individual that he is doing something for someone whom he cherishes and who appreciates him as an individual person. Social feelings, although not directly relevant to the object-oriented enterprise, must be incorporated into it secondarily to give it extra cohesion and continuity.

The nomadic hunting band has a different principle of cohesion than the group formed merely to satisfy gregarious impulses. It was in the context of hunting that the first *contractual* bond was formed. The hunting band forsakes instinctual relations in favor of contractual ones. It forms itself in the context of a relationship with an "alien" objective. The hunters can orient themselves toward their objective or target only insofar as they have to some degree released themselves from the closed sphere of personal and instinctual social relationships. The abstract symbols appropriate to the object and objectives entail an opening of the social instincts. To say that men form ties in the context of the objective means that their bonds are essentially symbolic and abstract, that is, mediated. The object which is their basic reason for association is also the mediator. The men's goal as an actual or symbolic presence must stand between them as mediator to offset the ambivalence and indifference of disrupted social relationships. Conversely the social relations must loosen in order to permit intrusion by the objective. There is obviously the danger that the objective or the object as an abstraction will interpose itself so assertively that instincts lose all continuity, rendering the object indispensable not only for material sustenance but for "social" integration.

The objective can stand between men as a *pure symbol* without reference to any immediate empirical fact. Not all object-oriented associations have immediate and pragmatic ends. But where such purposes are lacking there

must be an artificial purpose. This is the general significance of the ritual and the ritualistic group. The absolute
symbol, entirely without an external reference, is a mediating agent which stands in the place of the objective and
opens the man to it. Ritual groups are thus potentially
action-oriented groups.

All abstract ideas are obviously or esoterically mental
representations of the object. The act of visually fixing
an object has a corresponding cerebral process which is
symbolic and abstract. Such a process may in higher beings eventually become at least partially detached from
initial empirical stimulation. The idea is absolutely free.
Therefore we may speak of the object (or objective) and
the abstraction interchangeably in terms of their mediating function.

Language as symbolic communication is the *social* form
of the object in the object's mediating role. Anticipating
the argument to follow in later chapters, the monotheistic
god of world religions is the emotional symbol of the abstraction in its mediating significance. Hence the inner
identity of language and the highest god: "In the beginning was the Word, and the Word was with God, and
the Word was God."

The fact remains, however, that even though we may
define man's humanity in terms of his capacity to mediate
man-thing and man-man relationships, the mediative
ideas, like empirical objects and even like the targets of
the nomadic hunting band, are as such distant, aloof,
alien, impersonal and, finally, even hostile to the instinctually cohesive social group, the *res communitas*. Alliances
and associations for pragmatic purposes are not essentially social groups. They may actually extirpate and replace such groups. The principle of mediation tends to
translate the man as well as the thing into its own abstractness. The theoretical principle to emerge here is:
mediation is a condition of alienation.

Although man was the first being to develop a polarity

between base camp and hunting camp, between the family group and the masculine hunting band, the hunter had to return to the base camp—that is, *to instincts*. He had to reanchor himself in primal existence. Else he would have become a rootless drifter.

IV

MEDIATION VERSUS CULTURE

What a man does best he does for himself! I am not speaking of raising his "standard of living," which is a commercial catch phrase. Implied here, rather, is the production of those things which became an *intimate* part of a man's life. A man takes greatest care in doing or making what he will contain within the sphere of his own life, either as private property or the property of his community. An entire group sponsors with greatest enthusiasm those things which will become a part of local culture. Things of esthetic excellence and quality are kept within this culture. Therefore, insofar as culture is a few communicating individuals keeping what they do for themselves, it is basically antithetical to cosmopolitanism and the so-called "culture of mankind." Real culture is not for export. In fact where productivity is primarily for commercial relations with remote places, it is inevitably trivialized and made bland.

Culture is the personalization of what I earlier called the objective or object. Culture overcomes the initial foreignness of the pragmatic object, closing the man and object together and thus closing *out* men irrelevant to the relationship. Culture is refined according to the greatness, subtlety and passion of the person's esthetic perceptions and instincts as they find expression in and involvement with the objects of his world. Commerce, on the other hand, or any abstract mediative or distributive system, in releasing the object from the sphere of the person in order to transfer it to another human sphere, and in thereby *opening* the man-thing relationship, re-alienates, so to speak, the thing from the individual man. Commercialism is in this sense the antithesis of culture.

As an abstraction money, the medium of trade, is universal. The consumer product, insofar as it is reducible to money, is also a universal and uniform quantity. Marx called money the "spirit" of production capability. But as a pure abstraction, consumer "culture" is organically empty. What is done entirely for an abstract and alien "other," but not for oneself, is only very exceptionally, if ever, the work of love. High culture springs primarily from the work of private esthetic involvement. Mere commerce on an impersonal market, on the other hand, is a fundamental contradiction of culture.

As Oswald Spengler remarked of Germany, the culture of a people is fostered rather than hindered by the fact that the people is hemmed in and its culture contained. Defeat in war sometimes prevents a society from scattering and dispersing its culture, which sinks deep roots and continues to be nourished by its primary source in a region of limited population. It is not carried off and squandered in alien places. The rich literary tradition of the American South, the painting of Holland and even the metaphysics of Germany are works of high art contained within certain bounds. Even the mountains of Greece may have forced a concentration of effort in that region. Greece, in radical opposition to "world cultures" or "Phoenician culture" of mass commercial systems and ideologies—for that matter, in opposition to Judeo-Christian tradition as *world* religion—was a specifically regional culture. The containing boundaries of a culture, political or geographic boundaries, may be thought of in spatial terms like the frame of a picture which delimits its primary and fundamental form.

This is not to say that artists and philosophers do not

profit greatly from extensive travel and life abroad, or that cultures cannot learn from one another. Nevertheless the energies and purposes of a people must be attached to and accumulated within the particular regional and racial soil of the people. A culture of "being-between" could only be a vacuous abstraction. Yet commercialism promotes this generalization, calling "higher" what is only most general and universal.

A land inhabited by an instinctually cohesive and culturally complete people is a *region*. A region is a total cultural landscape which thrives only within the framework of its appropriate horizon, whether this boundary is set by something within the people or something outside them—a mountain range, a sea coast or a hostile neighboring nation. Otto Bollnow asserts: "It is just as true in the spiritual realm that the [limiting] horizon is by no means merely a regrettable barrier but a necessity of life itself, because it brings life together as the unity of a definite form. Without the horizon, life must flow asunder (*zerfliessen*). Peursen had also emphasized this point: 'Every cultural work recognizes boundaries which give it a place. A thought system exists only thanks to these barriers. They direct decisions, give points of departure, give determination, make points clear . . . All this can transpire only within areas defined by horizons. The horizon prevents a man from losing himself and gives him the means to determine his situation and to plan the way of his spirit.' Thereby the unruly and undisciplined expansion of the spiritual horizon, particularly through an externally and superficially appropriated knowledge that is not oriented vis-à-vis the individual's middle-point—such expansion can endanger the natural security of life. In his own time Nietzsche had in mind this idea concerning the dominance of historical knowledge. He emphasized that 'every living being can grow healthy, strong and fruitful only within a horizon'." [1]

The spontaneous form of culture, precisely because it

is confined to and contained within close social relationships, is not drained off but is quietly cultivated and distilled as it waits for formulation. Race and the home landscape—the motherland, *Heimat, patria chica*—are together, inseparably, the basic condition or soil of cultural creativity. Far from detaching himself from his race, the true artist draws upon it for energy, direction and, of greatest transparency in the artistic production itself, a sense of form. Ortega, who was not a regionalist or populist, said: "Blood, language, and common past are static principles, fatal, rigid, inert; they are prisons." [2] Yet Ortega was speaking here specifically of the enterprise of building abstract states, which, as he defines the term state, is a trans-racial endeavor. His sense of the creative elite is the super-national statesman and politician, not the regional aristocrat, artist and philosopher, a type of man of which Ortega himself was an example. It would seem that the forms of culture are true and necessary, organically spontaneous and self-evident only where there is *real form in personal relationships*, a coherence possible only among men of like race and region.

The oppression of a culture by the censorship of bureaucrats and priests may kill it. But its dominance by an aristocrat who understands his people may be responsible for its accumulation of strength and vitality. It was suggested somewhere by Golo Mann that German metaphysics was a deliberate attempt to obscure the expression of radical ideas in order to evade the censor. Following this principle of containment, there is nothing more fatal to a culture than an instant outlet, an immediate transportation. There is nothing more injurious to it than translation into the terms of transportation—money. When a people breaks over its restricting boundaries prematurely and devotes its energy to distributing its culture wholesale, it dissipates its culture. In destroying the limitations placed on it, culture breaks down its delimitations. Hellenistic civilization was diffused meaninglessly in the wide void of Asia and Africa. The most poignant example of cultural squandering was ancient Sparta. When all Greece had been conquered, Sparta simply ceased to exist as a special culture; it was left to old people and women as the Spartan victors dispersed their efforts in petty politics abroad.

The triviality of American commercial culture today, including the "arts," is undoubtedly due in part to its instantaneous outlet through the mass communications and commercial media, which carry it to diverse and indifferent peoples throughout the world. A "big name" writer or producer has his work spread far and wide the moment the most casual idea is submitted. The entire enthusiasm and force of commercialism is given not to the cultivation of an idea but the distribution of it. Moreover, the mediative system is one-way and the writer does not receive criticism from his readers. "Criticism" by professional critics is simply an extension of the distribution system designed not to deepen art and writing but to promote circulation.

In America it has been precisely the *freedom* of ideas and their acceptance for immediate and unquestioning export and consumption that has rendered them flabby and, in the last result, defenseless. They have dissipated their energies in utter repetition and stale mass production, confident of themselves because they have only themselves to listen to. The only limitation on ideas is that they must be programmed for the mediation system, that is, they must be liberal ideas insofar as the medium itself is liberal in conception. Consequently, "provincial" ideas are regarded by the media as irresponsible not simply from an ideological standpoint but from the standpoint of the mode of communication. It is in these terms that the new American *tyranny of freedom* can be defined. In essence the fact remains that the cosmopolitanism of the mediative establishment is the depletion and exhaustion of culture rather than its fulfillment.

It is possible in these terms to talk of an elite regionalism or elite provincialism. This is the molding and refinement of a regional folk culture, a living historical growth out of a particular soil, to the point that it raises itself above surrounding cultures. Elite regionalism is a long term development within a certain space of land and among closely communicating individuals—a development which nonetheless still has the rich content of feeling of the folk culture in which it is rooted. "Humanity," on the other hand, has no definition and no true form—for this reason, no culture. It is necessary to distinguish between *form* and disembodied *structure*. Form is a disciplined coherence of a definite organism; structure is a pure abstraction. Mass civilization is "culture" that is artificially abstracted out of a regional context to be transported universally. It is released from the fundamental conditions of its origin, that is, a delimiting horizon, within which a creative elite finds form in its communication. "Human culture," whether it be a trade network or the abstract ideology of world religion, is let loose to ramble with careless banality, assisted today by mass communication and transportation technology. Utterly opposite is regional culture. A particular high provincial culture grows only in a certain regional soil nourished by a certain limited segment of mankind. Examples are the Nürnberg of Dürer, the Mississippi of Faulkner, the Athens of Plato, the city states of Leonardo and Rembrandt. It is precisely the "freedom" and universality of modern democracy which would destroy these necessary boundaries and horizons.

A culture attains greatness when it contains its own productivity—or rather its ideas and energies for productivity—over a period of time. What originates in a certain place comes to be what its people want, nothing more or less. Where a work of culture is precisely to a man's taste and cannot be obtained elsewhere, he will not be separated from it. He not only creates the thing;

he lives through it. Doing and consuming are fused in an act of esthetic involvement. Does a man feel fulfilled in doing work which he cannot experience as a part of his own life? Or as part of the life of his immediate community? While no man can make or do for himself all the things he needs, truly creative work in a superior culture is seldom if ever done by a man who has the abstract intention of entirely *alienating* the work from himself. To promote work for mere abstract credit demands that the community re-enforce individual motives with such surrogate social values as duty, responsibility, the good of one's fellow man and "the greatest good for the greatest number." All these values follow commercialism around as its social conscience. Robot workers deriving their entire reason for existence from these invented concepts perform everywhere in modern society, but seldom with any joy. The alternative to the indoctrinated sense of public duty is to chain the worker to his machine or desk. Concepts such as work, productivity, product, consumption and utility are all transcendental cogitations which in a fragmented society of unstable personalities have come to replace the primordial fact of a man's total artistic and personal involvement with the things that naturally arouse his curiosity and esthetic pleasure.

V

MONEY AS MEDIATION

It was the international wanderer Marx who observed the wandering tendency of money: "Nomad races are the first to develop the money form, because all their worldly goods consist of movable objects and are therefore directly alienable; and because their mode of life, by continually bringing them into contact with foreign communities, solicits exchange of products."[1] The idea that money appeared first among nomadic pastoralists is also supported by the fact that cattle are most widely used among primitive peoples as a standard of value. Hence the Latin for money, *pecunia*, is derived from *pecus*, cattle. Now where nomads did not commit themselves as an aristocracy to particular regions, they turned to trading. In the barren and cramped areas between places of great civilization the nomads, who herded goats and sheep more often than cattle, could not accumulate sufficient strength of numbers and did not have the freedom to devise tactics of mobile warfare. Their strategy for power was therefore to embrace the abstract idea of militaristic nomadism as symbolized by money.

Nomadism with its patriarchal family organization, its mobile and rootless life style and its oscillation between raiding and trading is the prototype of advanced commercialism. Where life is uprooted, property must above all be *light* and not more than can be carried by horses and carts. Wanderers take with them the barest everyday needs—the warriors their weapons, women a few utensils. Like other mobile predatory animals they are not rich in children. While agriculturalists can let massive temples and fortifications accumulate opulently around them and can support great populations, the nomads are by comparison the rudest barbarians. But what these men lack in cultural mass and weight they make up in sheer force of arms. They exert themselves through sophisticated military strategies and technological inventiveness.

The most important cultural contribution of the steppe barbarians was a complex system of warfare which centered around the chariot. Spengler says that three factors were important in the invention of this machine: the conception of speed; a refined harness; and the training of warriors with specialized projectile weaponry. Spengler says that with the development of this system of warfare, "speed as a weapon . . . entered the history of war, and likewise [entered] the thought that the weapon-handy professional fighters are a class, and indeed the most distinguished class of people." [2]

It has been customary for scholars to distinguish two distinct cultural developments in the Near East—grassland barbarism and rooted agricultural civilization. H. G. Wells says: "The two ways of life specialize in opposite directions. It was inevitable that nomad folk and the settled folk should clash . . . Down pour the united nomads on the unwarlike, unarmed plains, and there ensues a war of conquest. Instead of carrying off the booty, the conquerors settle down on the conquered land, which becomes all booty for them; the villagers and townsmen are reduced to servitude and tribute-paying, they become hewers of wood and drawers of water, and the leaders of the nomads become kings and princes, masters and aristocrats." [3] This barbarism, however, can be called creative to the same degree it is predatory because, while through it a class or caste system arises it also creates a higher order, symmetry and organic cohesion for society,

conditions which are necessary for true culture. The nomads compromise and sublimate their mobility and the
abstract tendencies in their predation in the task of im-
parting definite form to otherwise amorphous peasant life.
They mold the peoples to which they commit themselves.
Of course they retain more than a trace of their former
barbarian habits in their interest in global exploration and
even, as Spengler asserts, in their "Faustian" space-
sensitive landscape painting and such obscure endeavors as
mountain climbing and aircraft engineering.

The steppes were relatively unsuited for agriculture
but they would allow great cultural potency to accumulate to vie with sedentary civilization. The greater nomadic peoples appearing on the vast grasslands could enter
into sudden alliances and overcome inert and defenseless peasants, imposing themselves as nobility. But always
this new relationship between nomads and agriculturalists,
while it began in the predatory exploitation of one people
by another, rapidly became a creative bond of direct and
concrete cultural and racial assimilation.

As nomadic hordes and civilizations underwent great
efflorescence and in expanding came in contact with one
another, a *third* way of life arose to soften the impact of
this contact. This way of life—it is better called a plan or
strategy for survival than a true culture—was limited by
material resources in its ability to develop an independent
existence. On the other hand, located as it was in the
deserts adjacent to and between civilizations it could also
mediate between them. The goatherd who was neither a
successful pastoralist nor agriculturalist became a go-
between whose religion brought reconciliation, and the
trade that is made possible by reconciliation. It was no
coincidence that the reconciler happened to have the
monetary wherewithal for this trade.

The eastern end of the Mediterranean has been such
an "outside" territory vis-à-vis the civilizations of the
Near East and, finally, Western regionalities and classes

in general. From this land come the greatest commercial and religious associations. For instance, the Mediterranean coast adjoining Judea was the homeland of the Phoenicians, who, like their neighbors the Hebrews after them, became a powerful commercial force. This land was largely a wasteland but had the strategic importance of being between the civilizations of the Tigris-Euphrates and the Nile. H. G. Wells says: "Across it Egypt, and whatever power was ascendant in the north, fought for empire; against its people they fought for a trade route. It had itself neither the area, the agricultural possibilities, nor the mineral wealth to be important. The story of its people that [the Scriptures] have preserved runs like a commentary to the greater history of the two systems of civilization to the north and south and to the sea peoples to the west."⁴ Correspondingly this middle ground has contributed the world's greatest mediators in a general sense, not only the most influential traders but also the greatest religious leaders with the *social* doctrines of human unity, which invariably follow and support mass commercial systems, particularly in times of the decline of the political support for such systems.

The Phoenicians were originally Canaanites, Semites related racially and linguistically to the Hebrews. Like the Hebrews they became racially mixed as they extended into other lands. Their principle of group identity was ultimately less a racial and cultural one than a common language and religion. Other than these two traits little remains in art and literature, or culture in any sense, that can be called distinctively Phoenician. The "art" of the Phoenicians consisted in imitations of the styles of adjoining peoples for purposes of commercial export. Darlington says: "[Phoenician] ideas were largely secondhand. Their art was largely second-rate, more valued . . . for the price than the possession. Their literature has failed to survive and this is not just that papyrus is perishable but that no one . . . was concerned to preserve it . . ." [5] The lack of cultural and racial cohesion was compensated for, then, by commercial profit. This same trans-regional Phoenician principle was the mediative contact by which diverse regional cultures could, in turn, trade and settle disputes.

The lesser nomads, the goatherds of the deserts of the Near East, could exist and rise to wealth and prestige only by *abstracting* their life style. These people became mediators—traders and religious reconcilers wandering back and forth between the great civilizations; and also living along the route between them and, for that matter, living within the civilized cities. Now where the forceful grassland barbarians imposed themselves as an aristocracy but temporarily lacked rapport with the peoples they conquered they set up a mediator caste from the outlands between themselves and the indigenous people. These mediators, even if they had to be captured by force and imported into the towns and cities, could render valuable service precisely because for their part they resented direct inclusion and, on the side of rulers and native populations alike, were never intended to be included in the culture on serious terms.

It was therefore not the nomads of the great grasslands but the goatherds of the desert who evolved the idea of money as an abstract force and also the idea of money's "social conscience"—world religion. When cultures wanted contact they were often willing to submit to a more theoretical or "holy" leadership which, although lacking real or enforced authority, did offer promise of a higher human unity. By the same token a barbarian warrior, contemplating the possibility of a kingdom of otherwise scattered and provincial peasants, could extend a kind of symbolic or religious equality to the people which would be the first step of a political unit.

In his book *Yankee City* [6] W. L. Warner describes the personal employer-employee relations in an Eastern

United States factory town in the 1930's. The small community, although stratified according to ethnic immigration patterns, was still an extension of a *res communitas,* a spirit of essential family solidarity. Or rather this spirit was gradually beginning to take hold. However, the factories were eventually bought out by New York speculators in accordance with the progressive centralization of money. Accompanying the trend toward absentee ownership was a demoralization of the work force, which became militantly unionized. Signs of deterioration of community life were evident in, and for Warner symbolized by, the felling of large oak trees which had lined the streets in front of the patrician mansions. The purpose of this destruction was the widening of the streets for the intrusion of the automobile. This was accomplished against a background of political rhetoric.

Warner, however, was in no sense regretful of this trend. He said that *if a world government is finally to be accomplished the groundwork can perhaps best be prepared by a world money empire.* Warner has correctly seen the impact of money, which, like the symbols of world religion, is universal. Universal money lays the fundamental structure for the world political order. Commercial materialism and its world market underlie a "culture of mankind." Warner saw that the tribal tie which resists such absolute systemization may be demoralized by finance and "Phoenician culture." Even an Anglo-Saxon artist like Booth Tarkington, in his novel *Alice Adams,* attacked the small-time and small-town regional aristocracy, although the only alternative at that time was a cosmopolitan de-tribalized and abstract plutocracy.

It should be understood that Warner, like Marx, directed his hostility toward capitalism *as culture* but not as a system of money. He viewed capitalism as it should be viewed, namely, as a regional and historical development like any other cultural form. It emerged like other esthetic creations from definite roots in a race and land. The forms and functions of capitalism *were* esthetic rather than narrowly "material." Capital was committed to a specific task of regional culture. It was money for a definite purpose that was included in the definition of the medium. Capital in these terms did not stand between men so much as constitute an aspect of them as cultural beings. It is this organic dimension of capital that liberalism decries. The liberal intellectual resents the *personal* society from which he feels himself rejected. Regarding the question of the personal dominance of the natural aristocracy, Max Stirner says: "Human freedom is in political liberalism the freedom from *persons*, from personal command, from *rulers:* security of every individual person from other persons . . . No one has anything to command, the Law alone commands."[7]

For Marx money is the absolute and universal mediator. It is intermediary between human needs and their satisfaction, between life and its necessities. "Money," said Marx, "is the *real* spirit of all things." Marx's primary contribution was not scientific but ethical: he gave money a "social conscience." The thesis of the Marxists is this: the world society, an abstraction, is a definite possibility because communication through the medium of money, which today connects all men in a world market, *is a true social relationship*. That men in a trading agreement exemplify the most general human relationship, which is thought contractual in essence, is the "materialist" conception of society.

In 19th century capitalism the factory was for its owner and workers alike a felt, concrete world, *the* special enterprise with which their life was intimately involved. Their blood flowed through it, their health and satisfaction in living depended on it as though it were a vital organ. For the true capitalist, profits belonged not to himself but to the endeavor. But the worker no less than the owner was committed to his work. The technicality of "ownership" did not dull any man's devotion, since the factory was his in an inward, cultural sense. It can therefore be seen that Marx, who never escaped his family religious background with its preoccupation with "contracts" with God, did not see how any economic life was possible except through formalism. The polemic of communism seems largely concerned with this kind of technicality.

The distinction between capitalism and socialism is an academic and artificial one, although this distinction is a matter of heated controversy for hypertrophied and abstract economic systems. Where men do not essentially understand each other as personal human beings, where they are not members of some cohesive family—not a theoretical "family of man" but a limited instinctual group—they are preoccupied by so-called property rights, rights of trespass and so forth. In this connection it is evident that in America the obsession with private property is a facet of the problem of estranged social relations, particularly the distancing in the area of racial relations. Whether it be the space of lawn around one's house or the interior of his automobile—the motor car is conceived as a kind of tank or mobile fortress—his property *insulates* him from unwanted human contact. The *res communitas*, on the other hand, is less sensitive and anxious regarding definitions of private and public property. In a limited regional society, private and public domains need not be theoretically or practically separated. Nor will theoretical collectivity expand to absorb and replace private possessions or vice versa. Private life and public life tend to intersect and fuse, to become indistinguishable. Where men enjoy the company of one another they emerge from houses and cars into taverns, theaters and parks. Certain "public" spaces become private spaces.

The pride of workmanship and a commitment to a cultural enterprise is prior to and outlasts the abstract system of any economy, private or communistic. It cannot be instilled or taken away by any legal act of expropriation. Or, rather, expropriation would destroy the real possessor as a human being. Spengler says: "I speak of possessions insofar as they have in them the tradition of culture. Possessions mean inner superiority, distinguishing classes of men. Not much belongs to the idea of possessions: a small well-cared-for farm, a nice piece of well-made handwork, a small garden upon which one looks with love, the clean house of a mountain man, a few books or a print of old art. What matters is that these things have been transformed into a world permeated by personality. True possessions are spiritual; only then are they real culture. To reckon an item of property's worth in money is somehow a misunderstanding or a desecration. To divide it [among strangers] after the death of the owner is a kind of murder. But who understands that? Who has today eyes and feeling for the inward, almost metaphysical difference between possessions and money? True possessions are an extension of oneself . . ." [8]

What has finally undermined the essential cultural and tribal mentality underlying the Industrial Revolution is not theoretical socialism but simply the fact that industry and capital quantitatively outgrew the capacity of real men to understand them or feel them as extensions of themselves. Enterprise dissolved into the empty dimension of money. Industry was intelligible only in terms of abstruse models which are the domain of money-thinking monopolists and their "social conscience" in the universities and churches.

Both capitalism and socialism are fallacies if all they are is systems. The conflict between the two "systems" is not worth a drop of blood or even a drop of ink. "Free enterprise" is what the mutual fund speculator Bernard Cornfeld called "people's capitalism," as he sold pieces of paper to accumulate a fortune of millions. The prospect of war with communism to protect his privilege evokes in most people little compulsion for self-sacrifice.

Even in primitive society people often want to trade. On the positive side they want what someone else has.

But they must be willing to part with something they have made, which is a part of their personal property. The distortion and trivialization of culture occurs when they produce items with the full expectation of entirely alienating them, fully separating them from their sphere of experience and dominance. Needless to say time may be saved by mass-producing some small items such as soap and toothpicks. These things can be passed from one person or group to the other without adding to or detracting from the total cultural personality of either man or either society. But if culture is defined as what men do most perfectly because they do it for themselves, commercialization is a contradiction of culture.

For the goals of trade, men must have contacts outside their own group. Trade means to open a society to another group through the mediation of money. It is necessary to observe here that such receptivity to another culture is often highly valuable since it refreshes the people's store of ideas—although these ideas must be given new meanings and subjected to creative reformulation. More than this, the exchange is simply a trivial barter for the so-called basics of life. The reason that a culture resists opening itself altogether is that in doing so it sacrifices its inner cohesion and definition.

Commercial exchange means that a man *alienates* himself from the goods he has produced in a trade for goods that are *alien* to him, goods that were made by an outsider either for his own possible use or for a purely abstract and ethnically undefined "consumer." The present study proceeds from the assumption that distribution is relatively meaningless where the distributed goods have little vital meaning to people who create or receive them. Focusing upon the creative moment itself, far from profiting from dispersal, the energies of artistic involvement must be concentrated within certain provincial and racial limitations which by nature are xenophobic.

It should be noted that this "alienation" can be an internal feature of a society. But since the time of Adam

Smith, the division of labor has been sanctioned not only by classic economic theorists but by Marxists as the basis of material civilization. As for the culture problem, Smith did not concern himself with things of greater cultural richness than mass-produced pins. This is because the division of labor, which is the focal concern of Smith's political economy, is not directly concerned with production in general or even with the means of production, but with the integration and systemization of spheres of production.

The "idea" of the division of labor is specialization. This logically implies that each area of production is geared to generate superfluity or "exportable" goods—exportable within the unitary system. The workers must satisfy themselves with abstract credit, that is, money. Now if culture is defined as an organic intimacy between a man and the things he makes, the division of labor is a disrupting factor in culture. It can be understood as "planned alienation" as a companion idea of planned obsolescence. Following the definition of culture proposed earlier, a culture is most vital when men work to retain the products of their work within the bounds of their own life. Men who stimulate one another to creativity therefore resist dispersal of their energies in superfluous contacts with outsiders. The concern of the trader or moneyman, on the other hand, is to get people to trade by encouraging them to produce for one another rather than for themselves. Affirming the division of labor and trade as the *primary* economic facts, the trader promotes the commercialization of culture not only in contacts between nations but within nations. Separating producers, and producers from consumers, he is able to step in between them with money as a principle of mediation. Indeed he is able to interpose himself between separate dimensions of one and the same person—the dimensions of producer and consumer. The man so fragmented is able to achieve unity of personality only in the abstract terms of the trader and his "social conscience," the priest.

A qualification to the above analysis should be interjected here. The fact should not be obscured that there is invariably a strong continuity of unifying purpose underlying the highly developed technological and industrial effort of the modern age. This purpose could emerge only from the history of a particular and relatively homogeneous race. In this case, so long as the division of labor is built around the common purpose, it can be called culture. Beyond doubt, for instance, is the elemental racial factor called "middle Americanism" behind the recent feats in space exploration. These high exertions fulfill the basic condition of culture in that they derive from communication among a creative elite within the horizon of an historical society. The division of labor around this organic core is an extension of an ancient primitive cooperation that characterized the simplest North European tribalism, from which modern enterprises can be traced through the trades and guilds of Medieval and Renaissance Europe. However, the division of labor as an end in itself sacrifices direct interpersonal relations in favor of a *mediated* contact. Machines are the middle term interposed between man and nature. Money mediates between man and man.

At the point of contact between disparate and remote peoples and cultures there is money. Money as such, as I said earlier, is not culture but empty mediation. And the void or dead space between races is no less a dismal and cold emptiness simply because it is bridged by mediation; the bridge may indeed encourage the vacuum. It is only in intellectualist apologies for pluralism that the moment of exchange and "diffusion" could be made a center of human intensity. Since the mediator himself, as academician, invents the theory of culture as a kind of world-market or "culture circle," it is logical that he is the hero of his own story. He investigates and often accepts for himself goods and ideas from other races, often profiting materially if he can somehow create a demand for these things among the people with whom he lives. To encourage such acceptance he must translate the foreign culture into terms that are bland enough to pass into his own commercial territory; or render them in a way that disrupts internal cultural resistance. This means in turn to create a demand for bland or even demoralizing "Phoenician culture." Now the trader and professor and priest are all in the center of this chain of exchange. As culture passes from one people to another it must be translated into the mediator's monetary, scientific and ethical terms. On this level of abstraction, culture is not only uprooted but turns against its regional and racial roots as a transcendental "culture of humanity" which under the skin is merely a shabby consumerism.

Where there is trade there is the trader. It is unlikely that a man will trade enthusiastically if he gives his attention to production and creation. I have tried to make it clear that productivity and trade are not simply different kinds of activities but are in many ways opposite and even at odds. The one demands an inward containment of energies and the other demands their dispersal and distribution. The producer therefore gains access to the consumer through an intermediary.

Specialized traders are often characterized by some sort of paradox or inversion which defines their outside status. Between North Africa and Sub-Saharan Africa are the long Saharan trade routes crossed by castes of traders. These men who spend their entire existence making the desert crossing are of Negro race but, paradoxically, also of North African Hamitic culture. Another commercial group, the Phoenicians, apparently exhibited no special and distinct culture except for one practice which was the abomination of the Mediterranean —the practice of prostituting women and boys in the temples.

How is it possible to live in the gaps which in terms of culture are a void? Certainly some wealth or the quantitative goods necessary to support life can be siphoned off in the process of transmission from one productive center to the other. But this is an essentially abstract wealth, a materialized abstraction. The loss of commercial wealth, on the other hand, does not detract from a regional society, which simply regards it as unwanted superfluity. So the narrow concept of parasitism does not apply to the trader castes. Nevertheless if the trader is to live on any level there obviously *must be commerce.*

At this point the trader may cease to be *simply* a go-between. He keeps his stance in the margins between discrete peoples and cultures, *but also he begins to take a keen interest in the internal workings and impulses of these cultures.* The trader is not only one who trades when people have something to trade. He also tries to encourage contact and "stimulate trade." He may intervene directly in particular cultures on the grounds that he is "participating." He is first positive and flattering, raising the cultures in the eyes of the world and writing friendly and amusing descriptions. But his main objective is to gear the cultures for commerce, which means to level them to where they are universally intelligible and capable of "consumption" by the broad masses of humanity. High esthetic forms resist exchange in mass markets and so are extirpated and repressed.

Having little interest in trade as such, regional populations are nevertheless flattered by having their culture, even in its lowest aspects, translated into a "universal" consumer item; and so without too many misgivings they are willing to see what was once an organically self-contained culture *replaced* by its abstract commercial image. Too late do they realize that this is no longer their tradition but empty trade. In America, which is presently committed to the concept of pluralistic democracy and intense interregional trade, the life styles of intercommunicating peoples are transformed into the "Phoenician culture" of the mediator. Regions, which no longer produce what inspires their particular temperamental enthusiasm, are merely points on a commercial map. This universal "culture" is not *of* any of the regional populations but *between* them. And its values, as all "outside" values, are *inverted* ones. They give public sanction to the lowest element in man simply because this is the most universal element. Accompanying the dogma that "all human life is sacred" and "the first come last" is the cynical commercial insight that "no one ever loses money by underestimating the intelligence of the consumer."

The connection between universal ethics and money-mediated communication is not difficult to understand. Money as impersonal mediation is also *universal* mediation. First, in the money society "every man is as good as his money." Secondly, every man regardless of "extraneous" personal qualities, among them racial and ethnic affiliation, is functionally equivalent to and interchangeable with every other man in the abstract economic system. Functional equivalence and the indifference of money to personal attributes is translated in the viewpoint of the intellectual moralist into a positive affirmation of all human qualities that are *not* personal and individual, namely, the "general humanity" of a man. By virtue of his "humanity" the individual is given certain theoretical rights. His functional *equivalence* with other men becomes "*equality*." He has a so-called right to be regimented in an impersonal system "regardless of race, creed," etc. He has the right to consume all the mass products envisioned by the adman and sold on a mass market. Finally, the trader is hostile to refinements of taste and personal attachments to things which, in causing a man to keep what he regards as best for himself, retard the flow of trade. This high estimation and possessiveness regarding the individual's own culture the intellectual inverts into the theoretical right to be ordinary, *just* a human being. In aristocratic and artistic societies people expect to hear something more than that a man is a man (there are three billion men!). In the commercial democracy when a man

says he is a man he is solemnly listened to as one expressing the highest ideals.

The mediator, in order to unite some men in an abstract alliance, must divide others. For him the dread
specter is no more or less than an alliance which, in crossing across class lines and other artificial divisions, brings
together men in the natural bond of race and culture.
This in America would be a union of middle and working class whites, whites of the North and South, and
Catholics and Protestants.

There is true creative dialectic only within a living regional and biologically homogeneous society. *Organic
continuity is a necessary condition of a creative opposition.* Opposing principles must interpenetrate and inhere
in one another. Form must intersect with, and largely lose
its abstractness, in its appropriate content—appropriate
because the form and content have a common history, a
common racial past. What is true of society, where forms
and personal meanings creatively work within each other,
also pertains to the external productions of art in which
society expresses its unity. Wilmot Robertson says: "The
conditions for great drama are only ripe when artist and
audience are in biological as well as linguistic rapport.
Such rapport . . . is bound to be short-lived because
the era of great drama is usually accompanied by large-
scale economic and material advances which tend to soften
national character, sharpen class divisions and attract extraneous racial and cultural elements from abroad. To the
great playwright, a divided audience is no audience at all."

Again Robertson says: "Not only great art, but all art
seems to stagnate in an environment of brawling minorities, diverse religions, clashing traditions and contrasting
habits. This is probably why, in spite of their vast wealth
and power, such world cities as Alexandria and Antioch
in ancient times and New York City and Buenos Aires in
modern times have produced nothing that can compare

to the art of municipalities one-hundredth their size. The artist needs an audience which understands him—an audience of his own people." [9]

Hegel and Marx sponsored *an absolute logical dialectic* in which opposition is uncompromising. Clashing adversaries absolutely contradict each other. This dialectical structure could only apply to a society which has become as abstract as the model itself. Here the oppositions are really contradictions which cancel themselves out. They are sterile and mutually destructive. With regard to economics as with art, a creative dialectic is possible between upper and lower classes only because there is an underlying cohesion and continuity among them which is sustained by a common organic or racial basis.

The question of organic continuity was lost on Marx, who could never get beyond the formal Hegelian dialectic. He dealt only with the polar abstractions of the absolute mass-man versus the absolute money-man. When Marx spoke of the capitalist he was thinking of the international speculator. When speaking of the proletariat he meant the acephalous street mobs such as those presently roaming at will through the streets of the great American cities. In America Marxist dialectic would be represented by the alienated abstractions incarnate, the expanding colored minorities and the similarly expanding commercialists. These sociological groups would form a system of oppressor and oppressed. But these categories also support one another in an equilibrium stabilized by the mediator. In America Marxism aims not to supplant the money class with a working class, but to substitute a Hegelian-Marxist dialectic for the organic dialectic.

VI

RELIGION AS THE "SOCIAL CONSCIENCE" OF MONEY

The Latin word *religio*, from which we get our word religion, derives from *religare*, to re-link. Religion may be construed in these terms as the interpersonal tie which cuts across organic or instinctual groupings of kinship, tribe and race. The religious community as such is symbolic and abstract and well outside closely knit traditional groups. Yet in being outside it can also function as a mediator to span the gaps between these groups. Even primitive cults have this mediating purpose. Victor Turner says of the Ndembu of Rhodesia, "Membership in a cult such as Isoma [a Ndembu fertility cult] cuts across even tribal boundaries, for members of the culturally and linguistically related Luvale, Chowe, and Luchazi tribes are entitled to attend Ndembu Isoma rites as adepts, and as such to perform ritual tasks." [1]

It is evident to the most casual student of history that world religions have been mortally intolerant of each other. Division is as much a theme of the practical history of religion as are unity and harmony. World religion no less than paganism is employed—and thereby distorted—in the expression of national and racial causes. On the other hand, if one looks only at religious ideologies, it is overwhelmingly obvious that their theme is not only one of accord but of *universal* brotherhood. It is therefore "in the true spirit of religion" that priesthoods, no matter how diverse their ethnic and racial origins, try to work together to iron out those differences in belief and ideology that stand in the way of peace. Of course, if agreement cannot be reached the bickering may break out in actual warfare. But each religion asserts only that it is the means to *true* human unity irrespective of national and ethnic origins.

It is understandable that religions designed to mediate in limited and local situations cannot be entirely reconciled. It is perhaps in this "true spirit of religion," then, that so-called secular priesthoods of writers and scholars continually emerge to work out ideology that is progressively free of any possibility for division and discord. In 19th century Europe the secular priests found one formula in the ideology of Mankind. In this chapter I will discuss the general significance of religious belief, even where this belief is called "secular," as its ideal harmony and unity is applied to the problem of stabilizing real social relationships.

Religion as a symbolic link may assist in consolidating real political and economic associations or even in expanding them. Religion supplies a fiction of social cohesiveness to groupings that are essentially object-oriented, pragmatic and extra-social. No astute political leader is blind to this role of religion. The obvious fact that religion may divide people under certain circumstances—particularly as religions are "naturalized" by peoples and regions as a dimension of their cultures—should not obscure the essential purpose of a new religious movement—i.e., to unify men. The symbolic equalitarian bond may reinforce a hierarchical structure. There are divisive conflicts between superior and inferior castes and classes which can to some extent be overcome with an ideal of unity. But primarily religion helps to stabilize relations between factions, classes, regions and races which would otherwise have divided allegiances. In orienting themselves toward a single superhuman and supernatural authority, diverse groups are often more susceptible to a centralized human political power. For instance, the cities of the Fertile Crescent brought together, in a process called *theocrasia*, different pagan religions to make of them divisions or categories of a world religion. H. G. Wells says that Nabonidus ". . . built and rearranged temples and attempted to centralize religion in Babylon by bringing a number of local gods to the temple of Bel-Marduk. No doubt he realized the weakness and disunion of his empire due to these conflicting cults." [2]

In Sumer and Babylon mythologies were merged and the various gods and goddesses of previously quarreling tribes united in relatively harmonious families. C. D. Darlington says: "As the empire based on Babylonia grew, the priests added the gods of one city to those of another, extending the national pantheon. In doing so they would insist that corresponding gods were in fact the same god. . . . It was thus the continuing work of the priesthood and the framework of their religion which made possible the achievement of a multi-racial stratified society." [3] In Alexandria Ptolemy I directed another theological *tour de force*. He arranged the worship of a trinity consisting of a synthetic Egyptian god Serapis (earlier called Osiris and representing a series of different ideas and principles in the course of his evolution); his wife Isis, a cow goddess represented in human form; and their child Horus, who was Serapis reborn. In one way or another any god in the empire could be identified with one of these three. But the three were essentially *one* god worshipped by all the different populations of Alexandria, with the exception of the Persians and Jews who already had monotheistic concepts. [4]

In almost the same terms, Alfonso Caso describes the work of the priests in the multi-tribal Aztec empire. [5] When the Spanish came to Mexico, the Indians were first drawn into Spanish culture through the medium of the

Catholic Church, whose priests recruited their own ranks from Indians and Spanish alike.

But the political usefulness of a religious community assumes that its outlines follow those of an actual or at any rate a desired political society. If the religious group is too narrow, as the Christians were at first, the religion is persecuted. Indeed, the Jews and Christians have constituted communities that were and still are *both* too narrow and too broad. They have sometimes hesitated to fight for their political order against symbolic brothers outside it. The desire of political leaders for the conformity of religious boundaries with territorial boundaries is seldom realized. On the other hand, the ruler may see the universal extension of his national religion to people outside his realm as facilitating the extension of his political power. Usually, however, religion is invoked to save a collapsing system. Wells says that for the empire of Constantine Christianity ". . . was a unifying and organizing force. . . . It provided the only hope of moral solidarity he could discern in the great welter of narrow views and self-seeking over which he had to rule. It, and it alone, had the facilities for organizing *will*, for the need of which the empire was falling to pieces like a piece of rotten cloth." [6]

The alliance between ruler and priest is nevertheless a suspicious and schizophrenic one. In its underlying nature religion is in competition with a national political order. Even where religion and politics are functionally united in a single ruler-priest, there may be a tension between this individual's desire to extend his abstract power universally and, on the other hand, his urge to involve himself personally with subjects of his own culture and race and to personify and express their national sentiments, values and ambitions. Normally, organic and tribal relationships between ruler and subject and between the subjects themselves prevail against mere symbolic ties. Even economic and military associations and alliances, which are grounded in pragmatic purposes and as such are nontribal and noncultural, may override religion. Religion's failure to achieve absolute authority rests on its essentially negative or *compensatory* function. The appeal of symbols is greatest where the political order is de-tribalized and artificial, and where object-oriented alliances, although desired, are not grounded in mutual values and purposes important enough to overcome strong national, racial or personal antipathies. The social order must be reinforced with symbolic and ritual harmony, order and brotherhood where organic ties are lacking.

But in the short run the priest (or priestly function) may earnestly vie with the ruler. The power of the priest rests in the potent but nonpolitical and noneconomic influence *inherent in his role as mediator*, a power which may with greater or lesser precision approximate political power. The priest has a special influence and dominance over society by virtue of his standing *outside* the particular, discrete sections of it. We may in this connection look at the personality of the priest, who is essentially an outsider and one alienated from concrete, existential participation in his appropriate group. In primitive communities, in particular, he is typically an epileptic, homosexual or recluse. These institutionally defined "pathologies" cause him, not to be expelled from the group, but to be held at a distance in terms of certain personal relationships, while at the same time he is reincorporated into the group on a formal institutional level. He dresses in special clothes with tassels and bells so that people can see and hear him coming. He lives in a hut isolated from the other houses and outside the village, but located between the village and other villages, which he visits in order to learn their magic and language. A language unintelligible to his own people is ideal as an esoteric adornment to his magic. He is one of the few people who can understand foreign cultures, even if only on an artificial basis. As a "reject" and an outsider he is also an ideal mediator.

One who employs the priestly strategy for power usually at some time in his life separates himself, symbolically as well as actually, from ordinary society. Within holy orders the priests do this according to an institutionalized ritual. Religious innovators and prophets isolate themselves spontaneously and fully according to their individual vision. When Mohammed went into the desert, the Koran asserts, ". . . he, as do all men, had known and felt himself alone and yet not in solitude, for the desert is of God, and in the desert no man may deny Him." Wells says of St. Benedict that ". . . with a hair shirt as his chief possession, [he] took up his quarters in a cave in the high southward-looking cliff that overhangs a stream, in so inaccessible a position that his food had to be lowered to him on a cord by a faithful admirer. Three years he lived there. . . ." But this separation led finally to a renewed involvement in human affairs, though on a new and transcendental level. "[A] remarkable thing about Benedict was his political influence. He set himself to reconcile Goths and Italians, and it is clear that Totila, his Gothic king, came to him for counsel and was greatly influenced by him. When Totila retook Naples from the Greeks, the Goths protected the women from insult and treated even the captured soldiers with humanity." [7]

The more separate and estranged communities are, the more conscious they are of their distinctness and spatial nearness, and the greater is the importance and dominance of the priest. The priesthood takes root in the crevices and fissures of society. A sacred order flourishes when these gaps are deep and yet for some reason a contact is desired. The priest as the eternal outsider, whose frequent alienation and "deviation" from personalistic groups can functionally be called transcendence, creates his own symbolic and artificial community and invites everyone in. They come only when they have to. The mediating institution of the priest is built around his personality as an outsider, and accordingly it is an uncomfortable place for most people. Men are at home here only insofar as they are outsiders among other outsiders.

In even a regional religion there is an initial subtle tendency toward the transvaluation of everyday values. As a given religion extends itself more universally this inversion becomes more transparent. Already in world religion there is something "unnatural" about the evangelism of universal brotherhood and love. While the Viking paganism, whose inversion was minimal, saw its heaven Valhalla as including first the warrior who had slaughtered many of the enemy—even women and children slain as they huddled in a Christian church—the world religion Christianity would admit to its paradise only the opposite type—the man who "turns the other cheek." Paul made the religious inversion clear when he said: "And base things of the world, and things which are despised, hath God chosen." But it is only as this religious idea approaches greatest purity in the *ideology of mankind* that the abstract idea turns directly *against* life, makes every value in support of particular, individual and formed life a sin. Here the ideology turns all values upside down.

The Catholic Church owes its evolution to the fragmentation of Europe during the breakdown of Roman power, providing spiritual unity and harmony to compensate for organic disruption. This mediating role is still retained today. Darlington says: "The Church, by its education, its interest in scholarship, its hierarchical discipline and attenuated family connection, was able to give unity to its genetically diverse components greater than that of secular society. It was, for example, able to open the way to social promotion for the children of poor parents, as especially for the bastard children of class crosses. . . . The Church was able and willing at every level to impose its own interest in social harmony on the class conflicts going on outside it." [8]

To pursue Darlington's argument further, the priesthood of the Church, imposing a symbolic unity on a fissile European society, arose through the irregular biological crossing over the caste barriers dividing that society. The offspring of such caste cross-overs were defined as bastards by the prevailing ethos of the in-breeding groups, among whom there was little intermarriage. Not legitimatized, these individuals were dispossessed and estranged. But as outsiders they were in a special position to mediate. Furthermore the Church drew from celibates of all ranks of legitimate society. The celibacy of the priesthood set it apart from particular communities in which the inheritance of property and titles and distinctions assumed biological continuity both through the generations and between living members. The priests had no heirs and so could not become simply another clan. The priesthood's title, like the academic degrees and titles of today (the only titles and elitist distinctions allowed in modern democracy, since they do not assume organic and instinctual continuity), had to be gained by individual effort or, more importantly, ideological affiliation.

The symbolic harmony of ritual and doctrine brought the heterogeneous, variously derived priesthood into a special transcendental and ideal unity. This ritualistic status, while it separated the priest from regular instinctual society, provided a new mode of relationship. Moreover, and this is why the priesthood was supported by society, the symbols which acted as a barrier to organic relationships provided a bridge or artificial framework between groups which, on account of *internal* organic cohesion, were cut off from other similarly cohesive groups. It gave these groups an ideal "brotherhood of man" to compensate for unwanted regional and caste disunity which would defeat the practical economic and military purposes of civilization.

Islam, although not a "priestly" religion, was in its formative stage, through the example of Mohammed, a world-view of "reconciliation." Following Darlington, Mohammed illustrates starkly the universality and alienation which make a religious leader. He was born in Mecca probably of mixed parentage, his father and mother descending from separate tribes settled at Mecca, his father from slave ancestors, a status which leaves traces in interpersonal relationships even generations after manumission. Mohammed married a wealthy widow and traveled as a merchant to all parts of Arabia. It was the persistent stigma of past slavery and the cosmopolitan viewpoint which came from wide travels which supremely fitted Mohammed to be a leader of all Arabian tribes, or what was the same, a mediator between them.

Mecca had sprouted at a point halfway between Syria and Yemen, along a trade route intersected by the track taken by Bedouin nomads as they passed between summer and winter grazing lands. An ancient black stone called the Ka'abah marked the place where tribes could meet, trade and have games without fighting, the same practice as that of the Greeks at Delphi. Mecca was centrally located in Arabia and its population came to be a microcosm of the diverse elements of this area. By the sixth century a small temple containing the idols of all Arabian tribes had been built beside the stone. Pilgrims from all over came to pray together here. Mecca prospered.

But, the city was still a settlement of disparate tribes, each inhabiting its own quarter and engaging in its own special crafts and tasks. However, for the leaders of Mecca and for the heads of local clans, all of whom would have their city flourish, polytheism, the worship of all tribal gods together, had become a new universal religion.

Mohammed was a monotheist who worked to bring

unity to the tribes torn by war. He saw the attempt must be made at Mecca where the peoples met in peace. He told the men of Mecca how to be saved, warning them to put away the idols of their fathers' people and worship one God. The effect of the message was to attract a following which set itself off from traditional groups by, among other things, eating practices. Meat offered to idols must not be eaten, Mohammed counseled, so that Muslims would not eat with idolaters. The voluntary isolation was subsequently reinforced by the general populace of Mecca, who defined the Muslims as outcasts. They were now a community defined by persecution, becoming a nontraditional tribe or breeding group named Unmah, or Kingdom of God on Earth. The group was finally expelled from Mecca, settling in Medina, a rival commercial settlement two hundred miles away.

The people of Medina were divided along lines of Arab, Jewish and hybrid clans. They had no single ruler to govern them and appealed to Mohammed as an outsider to arbitrate their disputes. His success in Medina secured this town as a base for Islam, and from there he ultimately recaptured Mecca.

Mecca dissolved its tribal affiliations, abolished its ethnic idols and gods and became a universal Arabian city. The law of Mohammed's God replaced tribal law. From then on, Muslim expansion was achieved through a core group of original followers who polygamously took women of non-Muslims and late converts and reproduced relentlessly. Arabian tribal energies were absorbed by this new supratribal religion, which directed itself aggressively outward toward non-Arabs.

What is this elusive and awesome quality or essence of priesthood? The priest is primarily an intermediary. His symbols pertain to gaps in the cosmic order between divine, material and human spheres. The interstices of the life of the individual or entire society are rich in symbolic content. Anywhere there is a transition, particularly an insecure transition, there is energetic symbolic expression —in rites of passage, in marriage, in the greeting of strangers, in the sectors where diverse cultures and races come together. For instance, in rites of passage the adolescent boys are first separated from their society, shorn of the symbols of status; initiation or reincorporation into the community is accomplished by "inverted" symbols of female status and of inferior social position. For that matter it is characteristic of priests, who retain into adulthood an "outside" status, that they are marked similarly as "inverted" men. They are expected to be chaste, unacquisitive, humble and gentle.

It is important to note that, if the best priest is an outsider, the best religion is an imported one. Buddhism died out in India, the country of its origin, but flourished finally in China and Japan. Christianity flourishes in Northern Europe precisely *because* of, not, as Nietzsche says, in spite of, its foreignness there. A religion is per se "outside" in that it is built around the personality of the priest, who often goes to remote places to bring in novel magical rituals and foreign languages to use as esoteric cant. It is difficult to overlook the fact that this religious motive is possessed by even the priestly anthropologist, who can admonish his countrymen by holding up as examples of his own ideal the exotic primitive practices of which he has personal knowledge, or, more likely, of which he has invented a concept in accordance with his desire for social influence.

Where not only various individuals but whole diverse populations are trying to cement relations, the religion binding them is most successful when it is an exotic, foreign religion. The more the religious ideas become intimately familiar to the people, the less suitable the religion is to extend international contacts. Exoticism in custom and costume, far from being neglected in religious mythology, is therefore emphasized. Jesus, the outsider par excellence, was not only of foreign culture in relation to Europe, but of indistinct emotional and sexual characteristics. But as a man with whom few can identify personally, he embodies a certain abstract "humanity" and is thereby suited to "bring people together"—as is also the case with his "oriental" religion and his God.

It has been only in high regional art traditions, for instance the Italian and Dutch Renaissance, that religious considerations are subordinated to esthetic ones. This was the rise of what scholars call the new European secularism but which could also be called, in a sense, a new paganism. What differentiates world religion from paganism is not the former's monotheism but its universalism. Paganism mediates within a much narrower in-group. This consideration raises the proposition that art—high art—is in an important sense *opposed* to world religion and mediation. Art is not only national but nationalist.

Protestantism may likewise be understood as a regional self-assertion, or a reaffirmation of vital immediacy between a man and his world. It emerged as a spontaneous reaction to the artificial social principle of Rome, which was being spread by Christian missionaries precisely at the time that organic cohesion was most decayed at the center of Rome. Luther significantly made *mediation* the target of his venom—the priest as mediator between man and God, as dispenser of salvation, as interpreter of the "direct" word of God in the Bible. By allowing marriage of priests, Luther also affirmed their tribal and national instincts, their identification with a specific people and region. They were no longer outsiders. Catholicism, whose *raison d' être* was to hold together divisions of an old empire which had become wider, had attempted to intervene among the originally separate regions to the north which had an underlying biological continuity but never an abstract mediative superstructure, and whose vitality and freshness were precisely in this unbridged particularity. Life itself is particular and, in this sense, "tribal." Therefore Nietzsche could say: "[Disbelief] means something entirely different in Catholic lands than in Protestant ones —namely, a sort of insurrection against the spirit of the race, while with us it is a return to the race spirit . . . We North Europeans descend undoubtedly from barbaric races; also, with respect to our talent for religion: we are *poorly* gifted for it."

The present chapter is concerned with human relationships. Of special interest are the gaps and empty spaces which open when instinctual and pre-symbolic and "prelogical" communication fails. These gaps must be filled to enable a relationship on another level, usually an object-oriented and pragmatic relationship. Such symbolic cement is the proper domain of the priest.

Men have relationships on two fundamental levels. On the one hand there are instinctual and purely social bonds, whose purest example is the mother-child relation. There are also pragmatic relations, associations and alliances mediated through the purpose or objective for which they are formed. These contractual alliances, which are often organically and instinctually weak, must be symbolically strong. Such relations are often formed between distinct nations, peoples and races. But also within a social group the contractual alliance is the characteristic masculine bond. Insofar as males are object- or target-oriented, they have less instinctual social cohesion.

The symbolic and abstract relations are quasi-social ties which support diverse economic and military alliances. But they may also be asserted for their own sake as a kind of moral exercise. The priest's power lies in this intermediate symbolic world.

Men depend on the priest to cement with abstractions important associations without basis in instincts. Without tribal bonds men cannot have access to one another except through symbolic interstices of society through which they must pass on their way to one another. It follows that the more important symbols are to the relationship, the greater the role of the priest. His influence over the symbolic keys gives him an indirect power over men, whom he controls by controlling their relationships with one another. The priest cultivates an ideal realm essentially foreign to the layman, even repugnant to him since it is a world built for and around the personality of an outsider. But the layman must navigate in it if he is to make contact with men with whom a deeper, more substantial bond is impossible. The ruler or aristocrat, who feels more secure when exerting himself through force of personality, knows that in a racially and ethnically diverse realm, where men are not attuned to him, his personal power stops short and an abstract power must be substituted. This accounts for his alliance with the universal man, the priest. For that matter, priestly and political powers may be united in one man.

The positive role of the priest is in rendering symbolic mediation where tribal and personal bonds are lacking. But insofar as his direct power is limited to artificial groups, he is understandably tempted to create small human agglomerates which are not relevant to broader object-oriented associations. He also fears the establishment between men of instinctual bonds which render symbolic ones unnecessary. In short he fears tribalism and regionalism, the positive bond whose obverse side, the exclusion of outsiders, he decries as "racism." He may actually attempt to undo these deeper organic ties by creating artificial associations which destructively cut across tribal groups. A pastor in Mississippi recently told his white congregation (although with some trepidation) that a black man who is a Christian is more their brother than a white man who is an atheist. This assertion would challenge the membership to choose between symbolic affiliations on the one hand and instinctual ones on the other. On the metaphysical level, the pastor affirms the old Platonic conception that the abstract idea is holy and eternal and instincts are "corrupt."

The congregations listen politely. But in Mississippi it may be assumed that the ritual community will not dominate, disperse and supersede the instinctual group. The pastor has made a bid for power and lost, since his symbols cannot shake off the instinctual values behind them, nor can they be made indispensable to trans-tribal object-oriented associations where these unions are themselves not useful. Even on the level of pragmatic self-interest, attempts to bring Mississippi poor whites and blacks together as a voting bloc or social force, have failed utterly!

The priests and oracles at Delphi, where Greeks regardless of region and language could assemble and have games in peace, were mediators in inter-city conflicts. But in the war with Persia they read the omens as favorable to the Persians; their advice was to let them in as masters. When the priests were ignored, they could be bribed by the Persians as spies. They moreover directly agitated among the Greeks for submission, asserting that Greek defeat was inevitable. History has many other examples of priestly "reconciliation." Cyrus could conquer Babylon and overthrow the Chaldean king Naboned because the priesthood of Marduk was in agreement with him. Egyptian and Chinese priests had occasion to behave similarly.[9] This unreliable loyalty applies to "secular" priests, the university scholars, who profess strict ideologies and organize themselves in rigid hierarchies but stand between nations rather than for them. The last philosophers of Athens were a petulant and dissatisfied priesthood, as Wells says: ". . . when Justinian closed the schools of Athens, the last Greek philosophers betook themselves to the court [of Chosroes I of Persia]. . . . The philosophers found the atmosphere of orthodox Zoroastrianism even less to their taste than orthodox Christianity, and in 549 Chosroes had the kindness to insert a clause in an armistice with Justinian, permitting their return to Greece, and ensuring that they should not be molested for their pagan philosophy or their transitory pro-Persian behavior." [10]

Such disloyalty, however, should be understood not just as the envy of what Spengler called the priestly rabble but as a definite strategy for power which, far from being desirous of absolutely overcoming divisions and oppositions, fulfills itself in stepping across national boundaries and between opposing forces to exist there as a *third* party necessary for the existence of the other two.

The priest has another recourse in addition to setting up symbols as alternatives to instincts. He may deliberately disturb personal relations within his congregation, forcing it onto a more abstract plane of communication. Any distinctive outsider "integrated" in a group demands the same formal communication that characterizes relationships between separate groups. The "integrated" group is not simply a community without bars to admission but is one with a different structural principle than an instinctual group. "Integration" shifts the structural basis of the intra-group relationships from an organic to an abstract level. Within the subdivision the integrated outsider has lost his distinctiveness, since the original members now all are oriented toward one another in the formal terms of the priest or sociologist. The abstract group may now be ecumenically merged with still larger abstract systems, which are virtually without limit.

The priest proudly directs these ritual relations. Insofar as the space of a church is an organic extension of social relationships, these ties undergo a profound change in integration. The priest is no longer a solitary mediator detached from his people but consecrates the entire group as a symbolic vehicle of mediation. The group is pervasively "in Christ," although more in a social than in a personal and individual sense. The personalistic group is transformed into a ritual community dedicated to "humanity," a mediating purpose which is made more transparent when the concept of God, which always is burdened by traditionalism and ethnocentric imagery, is replaced by the pure abstraction of "mankind." The remaining question is whether the priest can sustain this highly abstract climate until the instinctual group dissolves forever. Usually what happens, if the outsider is not assimilated into the organic texture of the group, is that the congregation re-tribalizes and re-segregates itself in subtle and informal ways. The ritual group and the tribal group finally polarize, leading usually to the dissolution of the former.

Symbols and symbolic associations are arbitrary and alterable. The symbols, while they may temporarily take an independent direction, must finally return to the elemental fact of biology and race. Tribal groups involve the whole emotional and instinctual man, while symbolic groups pertain simply to his abstract intellect. If religion does not ultimately affirm the tribe, then religion and with it the priest are irrelevant to and even at odds with the spontaneous flow of life.

A crucial stage in the formation of a religious community is reached when the symbolic tie begins to channel organic energies. The group that has artificially set itself apart from others begins to feel *within* itself like an organic group. This naturally assumes that the tribal cleavages, across which the symbolic bonds cut, are not so deep that they can never grow together organically.

The astute priest develops his symbol world with inbreeding in mind. Darlington stresses the food taboos which in forcing a group to eat apart create the likelihood that it will breed apart. The Pythagoreans were a cult devoted to the worship of mathematical forms, but they also were forbidden to eat beans. This restriction was not so trivial, since it evoked the intimate social cohesiveness of people who share a dinner table. Circumcision is another institution promoting a distinct breeding group. Any moral code regulating sex, not only laws of inbreeding and outbreeding but also of modesty (or the conditions of flirtation), would do the same thing. This raises the inevitability that, if ritual groups do not begin to develop into breeding groups, the ritual group will fall.

VII

THE IDEA OF MANKIND AS THE ABSOLUTE SOCIAL CONSCIENCE

The "idea" inherent in all Catholic deities and saints is the human bond of the universal *civitas maxima*, the City of God. However, many countries have not only their own patron saints but their own Virgins. The "idea" in each of these is universal, but the people conceive of the saint as *theirs*.

Here not the "idea" but the tangible image *esthetically involves* the peasant with a higher but fully personal supernatural force. This is not a mediated relationship. It is by living with this personal religion that the Church as a "universal" power has managed to survive.

Monotheistic gods arose to mediate in situations of economic and political pluralism, which were also situations of individual and racial estrangement. Sumer and Babylonia already had their universal religions as hierarchies and harmonious families of the diverse tribal factions living there. The Aztecs as a warrior caste maintained a priesthood which "reconciled" the religions of the many realms under Aztec control. In the Congo, Pygmies and Negroes who trade, but have little in common racially or culturally, nevertheless participate together in initiation rituals and other rites. Allah was the symbol of unity among diverse Arab tribes. The Catholic Church was effective in holding together the *orbis romanus* in a time of political disintegration. Even Plato formulated a kind of monotheism at a time when the inward unity of his city state was rapidly dissolving. Where old connections are weak the priests will intervene, thus both reinforcing a social edifice upon which people have depended and, at the same time, raising the power of the priesthood.

One primary aspiration of prophets and priests has been to provide esoteric symbols which create, at least ideally, an absolutely indivisible unity of men. To this end, in recognition of the full extent and diversity of humanity, they have evolved monotheism. But has the One God fully overcome the fact of human divisions? Or by creating fewer barriers, but not eliminating them altogether, has He not sharpened the intensity of the remaining hostilities? God has never become an absolutely abstract mediating symbol. He might be called a "halfway" abstraction still largely immersed in the concrete particularity of national and individual life.

God has been universal in his aspiration but particular in his derivation. All human beings seem to vaguely conceive a highest god but they picture him differently, so that there is perpetual confusion as to whether they are talking about the same god. There was the god of the Hebrews and the god of the Arabs. There were provincial cults of North Europeans which became symbols of national causes, even though missionaries had broken down earlier pagan symbols. Dostoyevski spoke passionately of the Russian god and of the mission of Russians to impose this idea on all Europe. But the supreme god cannot be a symbol of universal mediation when peoples war over the question of how he is to be conceived. Indeed, there is a strong tendency for the idea to degenerate from what is only a halfway abstraction into a purely personal and individual feeling.

Individuals are ever inclined to believe they can communicate with their god personally and with perfect understanding, without mediation of the priest. The priests, especially rural clergymen, understand that if a belief is to be passionate it must also be personal. The priest or bishop who is removed from the direct involvements of the parish asserts the contrary. He derides and castigates religious provincialism, concurring with urban intellectuals in humorous descriptions of anthropomorphism and folk materialism. A smile is evoked by the idea that the peasants conceive of heaven as the abundance of things they pursued on earth. As Ernst Haeckel says, ". . . the Mohammedan Arab believes it will be a place of shady gardens of flowers, watered by cool springs, and filled with lovely maidens; the Catholic fisherman of Sicily looks forward to a daily superabundance of the most valuable fishes and the finest macaroni, and eternal absolution for all his sins, which he can go on committing in his eternal home." [1]

In formal theology, religion aspires beyond itself to absolute and unqualified universality. The god concept aspires to monotheism not only in a "religious" sense but in an anthropological one. Such a god would be elevated not only over the limited regional and tribal gods, as over the spirits inhabiting every tree and rock, but over every trace of regional origin. God wanted to free himself of every vestige of an ignoble heritage in the provinces among barbarians and peasants. In order to be *for* all men, the final god had to be *of* all men—that is, Man himself. Only then could the old god be truly universal, although, in order to transcend himself, he had to die!

The people could not understand the theological god, devoid as he was of all personal and racial qualities; so they forgot him. Deism, the creation of the pure intellectual carrying through the tendency of the theologian, completed the negation. In becoming devoid of all human qualities the deist god no longer concerned himself with particular lives, thus in turn losing interest for these lives. It was by virtue of a necessary world ecumenical process that the place of god was taken by the supreme concept of mankind formulated by Comte, Feuerbach and Marx. Anthropology no longer complicated religion, it *became* religion. The maximum society of Man became what Stirner called an anthropocracy.

Of course, the taxonomic species *Homo sapiens* was secondary to the moral imperative implicit in the concept of mankind. Anthropologists today hasten to point out in every textbook that the similarities between men outweigh differences. As priests trace ancestry to a mythological ancestor in order to justify a group's self-identification, to define the group as a group, the anthropologist traces the "family of Man" to a common fossil ancestor, when, in fact, Carleton Coon has convincingly demonstrated that the taxonomic species *Homo sapiens* derives not from one but five fossil races inhabiting distinct regions. Moreover, behavioral scientists insist there is no scientific reason for one group to consider itself superior to another, to separate itself or even distinguish itself from others. All in all, however, the idea of Man is not a scientific concept but a moral one.

Max Stirner anticipated Nietzsche in asserting that the ideology of mankind is the last metamorphosis of Christianity. Stirner says this final liberalism separates the individual self from the "essence of Man," raising the latter in the same degree that other religions raise their gods, and transferring a general being to a transcendental level over the individual being. "Whom does the Liberal see as his fellow man? The human being! Be you *only* a human being, then the Liberal will call you brother." [2] Following Stirner further, mankind is an absolute abstraction in which the believer worships the universal essence of himself.

But paradoxically the person found himself more alienated from his own self-image as Man than he had ever been from a god, whom he could still call a real person like himself. He saw only the most general outline of himself which he shared with other human beings. This was not only his most abstract but his most trivial dimension. Consequently it was precisely the idea of mankind which came with inexorable finality to separate the man from the sensuous, instinctual and archetypal contents of his psyche. However, it opened the individual to the universality of relationships—not, as I said, as an individual but as a Man. But the transcendental Man cared nothing for individual men any more than the deist god had cared for them.

This depersonalization was in accordance with a "progressive" movement of institutions to higher levels of integration and abstraction, ending finally in a world society of mankind. This society, which was segmented in Eastern and Western blocs, then began falling apart in movements of national liberation and civil wars. In the "progressive" 18th century, however, the halfway abstraction of god was replaced by the absolute abstraction of mankind, in which the god concept fulfilled its essential "idea" of full universal mediation. Since the idea of a supreme god had to die in the sequence, the elevation of the moral concept of Man was called atheism. But if religion is construed in the sense of *religare*, to relink, the modern notion of humanity was a purely transcendental and catholic bond.

Yet, just as the 19th century saw the total victory of the idea of humanity, so the last of the 20th century will experience a new and real atheism as the final development of the same idea. With the breakdown of the world society and the reassertion of regionalism, men at the passing of this century will be the most cynical atheists regarding "mankind."

VIII

THE "RECONCILERS"

The mediator is the person who in being between groups cannot be *of* them. How, or by virtue of what attitude or disposition, does one become a mediator? Essentially the answer is by alienation and abstraction. Estrangement in terms of rejection and disaffiliation from concrete personal involvements and from regional culture entails *a need for re-orientation on an abstract level.* A contradiction or discord in the personal sphere forces a man to find order and harmony on an abstract, ideal level. The private and internal model can be opened as a public, universal ideology of harmony and order.

Now entire groups, to the extent that they are self-contained cultural groups, are likely to be estranged from one another in the same way that the individual outsider is separated from his particular community. Therefore the individual's solutions to his own personal disorientation may be appropriate solutions to broad demands for interracial and inter-tribal accord.

In primitive communities the character of the most frequent mediator, the shaman or priest, is likely to be that of any outsider, sometimes an epileptic or homosexual. But the main concern here is a kind of withdrawal that a man—any insightful and intuitively astute man—may experience with regard to "existing society." He thereby acquires the marginality necessary for the status of go-between. The prophet withdraws from not only emotional and personal relations but from older "existing" abstract and mediative relations. On the other hand, whatever personal quality causes a distancing from society, it usually does not incite a community to kill or exile or imprison a man, but only to subject him to the very isolation he seems to desire. His condition is commonly regarded with perplexity and even a certain awe and respect rather than with alarm and anxiety. People are somewhat ill at ease in his presence and would normally avoid intimate contact. In tightly knit primitive societies, the mediator is defined by institutions as a paradox and inversion. As an outcast his sexual and age status and role symbols are inverted by the priestly costume which strikingly sets him apart from other men. Much about him, in the context of tribal custom, is upside down. He is expected to say and do much that is opposite of what is prescribed for ordinary citizens. He is regarded somewhat ironically as one who would cause surprise were he to show some common human qualities. Certain words and images suggestive of potent instincts are prohibited in his presence.

To compensate for his aloneness the alienated man turns his symbolic outsideness into a positive strategy for survival. Groups which are "outside" in relation to one another depend on him as a go-between. The community therefore holds the outsider within it—but on certain formal and symbolic terms. While he is outside on a personal level, he is reintegrated into society on a new abstract and ritual level. This formal integration is the same relationship, in other words, in which discrete communities interact with one another. The coincidence is put to work as the priest or mediator provides the terms by which societies interact diplomatically.

It is now clear why, as the priest's status as inverted man isolates him on a personal level, under certain conditions *the entire value system of society* is turned upside down! Such transvaluation usually occurs when discrete groups whose cultures had evolved in antagonism to one another suddenly desire cooperation and accord. In this case the values of courage, self-sacrifice and patriotism suddenly become irrelevant. The arbiter, however, does not content himself with forgetting these values, he must turn them around! It is through his esoteric symbolism that the priest makes his inversion righteous and moral. Sexual inversion and a kind of priestly buffoonery become the sacred mystery which conforms to the mystery of the world, specifically the "outside world." The inverted man as divine mediator inspires awe and respect and obedience in the dark void of inter-tribal and interracial contact, where tradition and custom are lost and insecure.

It is instructive in the present context to consider the outside status of whole inbreeding castes or sects. Such status is implied in the word minority. A minority often arises from a dislocation and re-settlement which, if often repeated, leads to a special self-consciousness and resistance to assimilation. A point is reached where the group ritually and abstractly defines itself as a permanent minority, existing by straddling between regional societies and between segments of pluralistic societies. Such a mode of life is uncertain insofar as the intergroup relationships are uncertain, since they cannot be altogether subjected to the will of the mediators. But it is mostly a viable life because any contact between groups can best be mediated through the outside caste.

The Christian priest or minister is an individual outsider to tribal society who ritualizes this society in order to mediate between it and others. The priest is a "transcendental" mediator with respect to the regional community. The Jewish rabbi is someone quite different, and indeed has an opposite relationship with his community. His purpose is to promote Jewish solidarity. He ritually defines his people and sets them off rigidly from others. Far from proselytizing, the rabbi instils a keen awareness of Jewishness which he reinforces with a stern moral code of cleanliness, sexual chastity and loyalty among Jews, or any precept that promotes inbreeding and group separateness.

It is precisely the *lay* Jew who is a "priest" in relation to his host nations. Having been deported and uprooted for ages from one territory to another, and deprived of territorial affiliation, the Jew has learned to identify with his symbolic and transcendental nationhood. As I said earlier, Palestine, the ancient homeland of the Jews, has itself had the status of a middle ground between the regional cultures of the Tigris-Euphrates, the Nile and Greece. It is also the land of the great merchant people preceding the Jews, the Phoenicians—many of whom may have converted to Judaism upon the destruction of their empire.[1] The question arises whether this area at the end of the Mediterranean has ever developed a high form of distinctive *regional* culture. Whatever the case, the Jew has evolved a trans-national, transcendental national consciousness which can only be a symbolic and religious consciousness. Jewry is a third life strategy in addition to the nomadic-predatory and the agricultural cultures: Jewry is a *mediative* strategy. The Jews, moreover, are monotheistic precisely to the degree that they are spatially dispersed. Their Covenant or Contract with God is essentially a contract with one another—a general formalistic agreement which moreover is readily adapted to particular business relations. Unity of religion—absolute monotheism on an ideal plane—compensates for regional and racial disunity. It is not merely that the Jews are one nationality or ethnic group among others that sets them off. They are a special kind of nationality or, really, a *condition*, a "people" oriented by an idea rather than by a concrete familiarity with a place and a sensitivity to race in the narrow biological sense.

The Jew exists in the "pores and interstices of society," as Marx said. But it is precisely this outcast status which renders him of value as a mediator. Being outside the tribal and regional nations, he is also between them. The Jew in his ritual status is reaffirmed when his mediating services are needed, and he is castigated and damned when they are not. The Jew is invited in when he is needed as an economic or political mediator and driven out when cultures close themselves to one another, since his efforts to stimulate contact sometimes tend to disrupt inward and organic cultural unity. When communication and material exchange between nations is frictionless, the Jew prospers. When this communication ceases, the Jew is ignored or shunned. It is particularly in situations where diverse groups must interact but have no historical or traditional mode of doing so, other than straight political intimidation, that Jews are called in as arbiters.

Regional peoples call in the go-between when they disdain direct contact with one another. But mediation consists not only of spanning between peoples but opening them to one another. This implies the disruption of internal, personal relationships. Each in-group must atomize itself in order to integrate itself in a system of mediation. All men become outsiders in relation to one another.

The mediating role is the essence of so-called Jewish liberalism, just as it is the essence of Jewish society. The Jew is conservative, however, in his support of mediating structures. He believes in the principle of formal law and the courts just as he believes in the Law upon which Judaism is based. But in order to make peace among factions he must to some extent open them to one another. Mediation explains the Jewish interest not only in trade but also in the communications media, publishing houses, universities, government social agencies and the courts, to which they are irresistably drawn by virtue of their deeply ingrained sense of caste mission. The Jews belong to humanity. Insofar as America is a particularly hectic cross-section of humanity, they are especially involved here.

That Americans have for some time not been able to get along together on a personal and instinctual level has meant that American civilization has become mediation and, in this sense, "Jewish" civilization.

Jewish history is a paradox of profound successes and sudden setbacks. The Jew's role in Poland is an example. In the 13th century Tartar invaders had burnt out Polish towns and with them the middle class of indigenous craftsmen and traders. Only a shabby and backward Slavic peasantry was left in the countryside. A handful of Teutonic Knights moved in to set up an aristocracy. But culturally and linguistically and even racially they were far removed from the peasants, with whom they could scarcely communicate. The nobility therefore resolved to build an artificial middle segment, a heterogeneous burgher class of craftsmen and tradespeople to form a framework of contact between themselves and the countryside. They invited in various national minorities, including Dutch, French and English. But the largest minority was that of the Jews, who had always been the most willing of ethnic groups to relocate themselves. As an inbreeding caste with a gift for trade and a history of straddling between disparate peoples, they were most successful as a surrogate bridge between the knights, peasants and whatever other groups were then living in Poland. They laid the foundation of a national structure among peasants in that they (the Jews) established a commercial structure. The Jews were the means to a new Polish national consciousness, although at first it was only an abstract and symbolic consciousness.

However, German and Polish Christian elements, as well as the foreign gentiles adopted into the middle class, began to coalesce organically while hybridizing racially and culturally within the original artificial framework. Discrete castes, while maintaining a sense of class identity, began to interpenetrate marginally. Illegitimate offspring of caste crosses formed their own hybrid but legitimate lines, developed into a middle class and further incorporated elements of both castes. These castes in turn incorporated the hybrid middle class. Eventually the Teutonic Knights and the peasants became the modern Polish people. What then happened to the Jews? As the Christian castes came together, the need for artificial and mediated relations between them ceased. The subtle, nonverbal, noncontractual understanding that exists between men who historically and racially "belong" to the same community, rendered unnecessary the symbolic and abstract ties supplied by traders and arbiters.

The Jews, as an inbreeding symbolic and ritual caste extending beyond national territorial boundaries, were simply frozen out of Polish society despite their former service. Their last task was to mediate between Poland and other countries, an endeavor which finally led the Jews to import international socialism. This function again became irrelevant as communism was incorporated into the organic and national life style of Poland, just as Catholicism had been "naturalized" earlier. The Jews, for all their previous assistance in times of transition, were simply packed in trains with a few belongings and deported.

Jews and the function or principle of mediation become "irrelevant" not only when disparate people grow together instinctually, but also when they irreconcilably grow apart. The Jews were the main mediators between the Spanish aristocracy and the Moors in Spain. The Spanish nobles had acquired a taste for the luxuries and scientific ideas which came from the Moors, who while fighting the Spaniards also had indirect exchange contacts with them. But since they would not deign to have personal contact, the Jews were always moving back and forth in the marginal zones between them. But the "territorial imperative" and the drive to found an organic Spanish nation triumphed over the impersonal, meta-cultural contact. The Jews, who in the eyes of Spaniards were representatives of the Arabs, were expelled along with them. This and numerous other expulsions and resettlements have reinforced the ritual identity of the Jew and have established his status as an outsider and mediator in his host countries.

America, a civilization of mediation, now poses the alarming possibility that a blue collar–white collar, urban-rural and North-South populist coalition will close in front of Jewry and mediation in general, excluding it as a social force. Various Christian nationalities—Anglo-Saxon, Irish, German, Polish and so forth—are developing a subtle understanding, a relative unanimity of instinct and nationhood deeper and more basic than a mediated "agreement." They are racially and culturally hybridizing across margins which had previously been transcended only through the symbolism and ideology of religious, academic, financial and communications establishments. The contractual terms once necessary to the relations between these nationalities are now barriers in the way of a deeper accord. The institutions of contractual accommodation have been secure only so long as personal relations were *in*secure.

At the same time, America seems to be dividing irreconcilably, not only organically but symbolically, letting the mediator collapse in the widening schism. The relationship between whites and nonwhite minorities, which has always been artificial, is increasingly insecure. The nonwhite minorities have been accommodated in a philosophy and social system vaguely designed by the white minorities for the purpose of harmonious relations with one another. The colored minorities, apparently in rejection not only of biological affiliation but also of symbolic unity with whites, have begun to establish their own ritual communities. Spurious Africanisms have begun to sprout. A celebrated mulatto entertainer who had converted to Judaism was more to the point. He asserted that his real religion was his blackness. This reactionary equation of race and religion means absolute separatism.

Regarding the much discussed "Jewish intelligence," the relevant factors seem to be sociological rather than biological and racial. The Jews are a race more in a statistical sense than in the sense of having internal and instinctual cohesion. If there is a "Christian race," then there is a Jewish race—although Christendom is a group of diverse nations, while the Jews are an aggregate of individuals. The fact that they inbreed, are gregarious among themselves and instil in their children a sense of belonging apart from any question of religious belief, does not raise them to that formed unity of population, land and culture which constitutes a race or *Rasse* in Spengler's sense. For Spengler, "a race does not migrate!"

Certainly, as Darlington points out, the Jews who did not cling tenaciously to their religion and way of life were absorbed into regional populations and lost to the Jewish community. This is still not to say, however, that the Jews are a true race. The "race" of the Jew is an ideal of nationhood in lieu of a real organic continuity, which has been all but broken in interaction and interbreeding with the various groups and nations with which he has had prolonged contact. Likewise his history is a "priestly" one, in the sense that the priest is one who sanctions a group identity with a mythological genealogy. It is precisely because the Jews are not an organic people with a felt continuity in time that they gave themselves and the world their imaginative history in the Old Testament.

The fact that the Jew is oriented in his social life by an ideal rather than by instincts has profound consequences for his economic behavior. His superiority in the latter realm is a result not so much of a higher intelligence as it is of his freedom from instincts, which allows him to specialize absolutely in an abstract niche. On the other hand, this astuteness is bought at the expense of a certain deftness in subtle political intrigue. The Jew has always been characterized by a certain theoretical sophistication which shows in crucial situations its instinctual naiveté. The Jew as a social group has been afflicted with the disease of all highly abstract institutions, namely, insularity in relation to the free play of collective instincts among the base populations. The strength of the Jew is abstract analysis. His weakness is lack of intuition.

The outsider is better adapted than regional men for work in systems of mediation, which transcend particular lands and cultures. The abstractly oriented man is not held back by tribal instincts. Where arbitration is a priority, the personally or ethnically "alienated" individual or group is at an advantage in competition. The outsider excels not only in situations of international contact, but in the context of social pluralism, where inbreeding castes specialize for complex divisions of labor. In pluralistic structures, centers of productivity must subordinate their efforts to integrative factors. Here the mediator (using the word in the widest sense), who does not need to be directly involved in creative effort, can rise to prominence precisely because he is *not* involved in particular enterprises, but rather is between and above them.

In more general terms, not only is the outsider competent in arbitration and integration as such, but, since mediation is an abstract activity, he is likely to excel in other abstract endeavors such as mathematics, "pure" science and the handling of money. However, in more concrete areas, not only in art and literature but in certain regional and national styles of science (Heisenberg suggests, for instance, that quantum mechanics is derived from traditional German folk science, or alchemy), the status of outsider is a drawback. The reason, apparently, is that art or any science depending on concrete imagery demands an active participation of a whole range of organic factors, from sense perceptions to feelings and a sense of intimate, personal social life.

By definition, pluralism is a system of mediation. The pluralistic democracy is led by individuals and minorities which, unlike specific organic groups constituting centers of productivity and culture, have mainly integrative interests. Members of supranational religious minorities excel insofar as the transcendental consciousness is itself integrative. The most publicized of these ritual groups is the Jews, but also highly esteemed are Quakers and Mormons. Among all distinctive American minorities the Negro is the only one who is not cast in the role of mediator—he is the person whom the mediation is largely about!

Of great interest are the former American slaves who re-settled Liberia after several generations in the New World. With a culture largely taken from their American captors, they had little in common with the tribesmen of Liberia. Yet it was not this new culture which made them dominant over the native Liberians; nor did race set them apart. Rather they took control simply by virtue of the fact they *were* outsiders who during their absence had had contacts with widely different peoples and learned English, which is the trade language of much of the world. Any relations between tribesmen and the outside world had to be mediated through the returned ex-slaves.

Therefore it is necessary to distinguish success in systems of mediation from achievement in self-contained cultures. A mediative structure is the abstract generality of all human culture. Such a system is not really a culture at all, since cultures are by definition particular and plural. In systems of mediation, values held in common by all men everywhere are sanctioned because only the awareness of common values overcomes human insularity. But whereas a man cultivates higher, more distinctive and aristocratic values in order to set himself apart from the broad mass of humanity, mediation affirms the most common or lowest values, the values that do not require self-discipline or special strength. These, then, are not just qualitatively inferior impulses but opposite to the elite ones. They are essentially the *denial* of form-affirming values. In the world view of the mediator, common values are a deliberate reversal, having, nevertheless, a self-righteous mission. Only outside values, like outside men, mediate.

A nonterritorial nation interposed between organically self-contained nations must be abstract. Life in the interstices, since they are filled with abstract quantities, taxes the abstract faculties especially. Here the Jew's abstract nationhood is of great assistance. He integrates himself into a realm of theoretical concepts, such as ideology and money, through the same intellectual abilities with which he integrates himself into his abstract religious society.

But the same ease with money and abstract values which so bewilders his regional competitors, also entails a lack of feeling for the raw matter and energy of the world, a sensitivity which is essential for basic kinds of creativity. The Jews are remarkably lacking in truly outstanding composers and painters considering their contributions in purely abstract areas of science, trade and ideology. This fact is underscored rather than disproven by the problematic and dubious exceptions. A painting by Modigliani, prints by whom decorate so many houses in "Phoenician" America, can be convincingly faked by an expert in one hour. Jewish song writers, dramatists and, lately, cartoonists have gained fame primarily by translating a common type of folk culture directly into commercial and urban terms, without, however, substantially rising above it. Jewish "culture," which is synonymous with "commercial culture," seems to be a kind of cosmopolitan folk art. But universal folk culture is a paradox. With regard to the much-publicized rash of Jewish accomplishments in physics and medical research, full evaluation must be left to the future when the journalistic enthusiasm of the moment has passed.

Freud and Marx, the greatest contemporary Jewish philosophers, exhibit certain inversions of the esthetic values of regional cultures. Freud says: "Many of us will . . . find it hard to abandon our belief that in man himself there dwells an impulse toward perfection, which has brought him to his present heights of intellectual prowess and ethical sublimation, and from which it might be expected that his development into superman will be insured. But I do not believe in the existence of such an impulse, and I see no way of preserving this pleasing illusion." Freud dissects the human being into the *abstract* elements of a mouth, penis and anus. Having the mediator's frame of reference, Marx makes all men into materialists, an image more attractive to the adman than to the scientist, not to mention the poet.

The Jews have usually been a little ahead of the regional nationalities in "creative" output. The exceptions to their superiority—but for the purposes here the only instances that matter—are the rare periods of voluptuous and impassioned outpouring, a blend of discipline and frenzy, which mark the highpoints of all human life. However, the regional peoples have subsequently undergone periods of painful decadence. When culture sinks from its most dizzy heights, the Jews are often the tallest among those living in the valleys. The Jews fill in where there is a vacuum. Their creativity either precedes or follows high traditions in art. With the decline of Russian literature, for example, one notes the increasing prevalence of Jewish names. In the Italian and Dutch Renaissance there were no outstanding Jewish artists. Today, however, many of the highest paid painters in New York are Jews, as is also true in literature.

Americans more than most other people have so far been unable to form the close instinctual social relations which are the *sine qua non* of culture. Among such people there is always something superior about Jews, who, orienting themselves as they do by abstractions, do not depend on instincts.

IX

MEDIATION AS THE LEITMOTIF OF AMERICAN CIVILIZATION

G. W. F. Hegel said of the French Revolution that it was the first time mankind "stood on its head." Hegel meant that at last men endeavored to freely organize society according to *reason* rather than passively accepting modes of interaction determined by uncritical, instinctual and tribal impulses. Man had extricated himself from the "enslavement" of evolved, traditional bonds and could now substitute deliberate, rational, thought-out bonds. However, in an important sense Hegel's analysis was superficial. While he correctly saw that the motives of the Revolution were ideological and abstract, that they ideally encompassed not only all Frenchmen but all humanity, he nonetheless missed the fact that the commitment of the French to the idea-based society was not final. The Revolution was simply an experiment of the Enlightenment. Whether the people felt themselves in earnest or not, the experiment, even when it was actualized in official national politics, was still a mere theory. Underlying the enlightened "revolutionary" society—revolutionary, that is, against instincts—there was still in France a deeper historical and tribal society and culture. They still had the security of this knowledge. No people could embark on the unfamiliar sea of reason unless there was solid ground within safe distance. Unless, that is, the ground was as new and unfamiliar as the reasoned utopia itself. Such a new world was America.

Not the French but the New World society would have best fit Hegel's notion of a society "standing on its head." American society came into existence upside down. From its very beginnings its primary basis—an energetic attempt to found a real American culture notwithstanding—has been the ideals and theories of European revolution and the Enlightenment. Mediating rationality was substituted for an historically grown-together society as the basis of culture.

Now this adaptation through abstractions rather than through direct life contact was understandable and predictable among people who were essentially strangers to one another and who found themselves in a new place. In this setting of initial unfamiliarity, theories and abstractions had to bridge the distance between people and the land and between the people themselves. In modern Israel the basis of the resettlement of biologically disparate individuals was the ideology of Jewish nationality.

The ideals of the Enlightenment performed this same role among dislocated and racially disparate Europeans in America. Abstract ties were substitute bonds that produced a pseudo-cohesion while instinctual ties were given time to take hold gradually. The abstract institutions of democracy were merely the scaffolding. They were never intended to be the building itself. Understandably the theoretical democratic order was subsequently amplified, since the artificial order has facilitated the settlement of great and diverse masses of men over vast territories. As these masses became more disparate, particularly as the Negro became a more conspicuous presence, the structures were amplified even more. They could be vastly extended by modern techniques of bureaucratic regimentation, electronic communications and computers. By the same token the builders of these structures identified with them to the extent that, like the Ottoman Turks, they largely sacrificed consciousness of their own racial identity while attempting to force others to give up theirs. If race is the basis of any enduring nationhood, it is therefore impossible that the theories of the Enlightenment are the true destiny of America.

Nor is materialism the destiny. America is perhaps the most materialistic of all nations. This is because of its newness. America was first construed as the *booty* of nomadic Europeans. Yet in becoming uprooted from their European regional social groups, in which solidarity was instinctual, the booty which was the objective of their exploitative energies had to become, paradoxically, the mediator of a new "social" cohesion, albeit a cohesion on an abstract rather than an organic level. The lack of mutual understanding and attraction among Americans entailed a need for a social juxtaposition, a purely causal and mechanical interaction provided by money systems. Money became a social gospel, not just an economic medium. Whereas in Europe economic systems grew out of historical and corporate cultures, in America, the land which was and is the "target" of European viking-style hunters, the abstract system has been prior. Economics establish the framework in which culture must finally take root.

Into the potential bedlam and anarchy of instincts came the historically institutionalized mediator, the paradox of the outside race which is not a race, the absolute nomad whose "race" is a statistical composite of every place he has been in his venerable history. He brought with him money and also the "social conscience" of money. These and the mechanical expression of these, the mass communications media, were terms in which Americans, foreign to one another as they were, could make contact. Therefore it has come to pass that to challenge not simply the "ethnic" mediator but the principle of mediation itself, money and its social conscience, is an *anti-social act*. Materialism, while on the surface it is simply an insatiable craving for consumer goods, is in its deepest essence a social orientation. The American often cannot perform socially except against the background of consumer goods, which he places between himself and other men as objects of attention and conversation in so-called "social" situations. The men do not have direct personal ties, rather they orient themselves around consumer items.

Economic decline or recession is therefore more dangerous in America than in other more instinctually secure and culturally stable lands. Lacking natural compassion, men are kept from attacking one another only by virtue of the necessity of material cooperation. The initial breakdown in a recession would be along racial lines, but the deterioration would proceed further to interpersonal relations. Hence the awesome power and status of the trader and banker keeping the consumer goods and money moving between otherwise isolated individuals. Were commercial wealth to concentrate in a few hands, the mediating function of goods and money would cease. Therefore, the priestly ideologist, socialist and human relations specialist give money a social conscience, distributing it "to all the people" and thereby drawing even the most estranged of all men, the poor and the black, into the circle of material mediation.

This is to say, in other words, money contacts are a *kind of communication* which, as the only communication the Americans at this time are capable of, must suffice until a deeper understanding has time to take root.

Now the elaboration and implementation of a so-called revolution, not only the radicalization of ideology and institutions but also the acceleration of middle-class materialism, was not, in the case of America, a real revolution but merely the pursuit of an established direction toward more abstract and universal mediating structures. Since in the American context upheaval means the opposite of what it meant for Europeans, the true revolution has not yet appeared in the external life of the Country, although it has long been under the surface. It would consist not just in a dismantling of institutions but in the negation of the universalist "ideas" inherent in them and the reversal of the *sequence* whereby institutions destroy themselves in order to display these "ideas" more transparently and absolutely. A true revolt for America would mean the overthrow of the anti-tribal, anti-instinct revolutionism wherein the society was forced to do an unnatural headstand. Society would regain its natural stance. It would establish fundamental organic relations among people and between people and land. Americans would spiritually and culturally incorporate with one another to become, within themselves, whole citizens. In an important sense America, which is presently the halfway abstraction of Europe-in-general, would become *more* European, if Europe is construed as a number of self-contained regional cultures.

X

THE END OF "SOCIAL PROGRESS"

Both dictatorship and democracy have advantages which suit these systems for different purposes. Dictatorship tends to bring order and efficiency to society, and is thereby suited to cope with crisis. Democracy, on the other hand, has a greater tolerance for the individual. To say democracy is superior to dictatorship is simply to say that peace and prosperity are better than crisis. However, no one would advocate authoritarian government when there is a possibility for personal freedom.

Nevertheless it is clear that given enough time, democracy can equal and even surpass dictatorship in suppressing individual freedom. Democracy may work against the person slowly, but the results in the long run are no less oppressive. A voting majority could potentially dominate a minority to the point of extinction. Democracy is sustained, then, only by the hope of the minority that it can build itself into a majority by the next election. The building of a majority from a minority depends on the flexibility of individual opinion, which is the basis of a living democracy.

This flexibility depends in turn on an underlying basis of agreement among the majority of voters. The person must feel that by changing his own feelings or influencing others to change theirs, he will sometimes be in a majority, if not in every election, then, say, every twenty years. If this rhythm turns into a static alliance of voters in rigid blocs, the out-voted person feels that the system is no longer "his."

Democracy decides issues by a concentration of ballots. All real politics ultimately comes back, however, to a concentration of human will, energy and passion. The productive and creative members of society, most of whom are white and have children of school age, inevitably have a basic and long-range political understanding quite apart from their voting habits and voting strength; they make final decisions on important issues. The old, the young, the weak and poor of a society *cannot* in the last analysis, by simple numerical majority, rigidly coerce and subjugate the solid core of workers and family heads. At most, the unproductive poor can exert themselves indirectly through a handful of resourceful leaders whose influence, however, is mediative.

The out-voted man, if he is an astute and determined man, if he finds himself working for others and not himself, and if the voting majority has little strength beyond the ballot, accomplishes his individual ends by abolishing the entire system and setting up a new one for his private purposes. He establishes a dictatorship. The difference between dictatorship and democracy in this case is the incidental fact that formerly a majority oppressed a minority, whereas now a minority (within which there may be great personal freedom) dominates the majority. At the time of the overthrow, the democracy was already dead and superfluous, since there were individuals to whom the system was a *mortal* enemy.

These individuals become implacable enemies of the so-called democracy and will not rest until the system is destroyed. They are right in assuming that democracy would eventually crowd them out of existence as surely as would the most pernicious dictatorship, and the fact that under a democracy this process might take a little longer is unimportant.

In America more than twenty years ago there were

crucial productive citizens alienated from the system. The estrangement was the consequence of bloc voting in which the individual identified his personal interests with those of his economic, ethnic or racial group. The system, although perhaps already desperately ill, at that time still had the lucky feature that the voters of the majority imagined themselves to *be* a majority. They were therefore satisfied with the existing system, while the voting minority pondered the situation and was meanwhile mollified by its economic prosperity. The delusion of the "majority" is today shattered, leaving each voter with the feeling that he is trapped in a hopeless minority and destined to be forever outside the system. One combination of blocs will win in every election. But each bloc will be conscious of itself as a true minority and may doubt that it can protect itself by protecting the system. *The fallacy of democracy in a pluralistic society is that populations that do not essentially understand one another are potentially uncompromising toward one another.*

A true and lasting democracy is possible only when men understand one another. When they understand one another they do not need democracy.

America presently has formal and institutional political stability *because of*, not in spite of, internal discord. Where there is a relatively homogeneous racial population, parties can only be *intellectual* creations, with ideologies that are often in radical opposition. The truth is that politics need not stress ideological harmony in a homogeneous state, where healthy internal politics have to do with issues, not races. This is why in America the appearance of new movements with strong racial consciousness, even though there is no clearly defined ideological viewpoint, is a grave portent of the future.

"Social progress" is the increment of artificial mediation in human relationships. Mediation is defined here as an abstract between-ness which fills gaps in the organic substructure of instincts. This abstract capacity, which belongs to human beings but not to lower animals, allows men to interact even when they have no personal or organic basis for doing so. Abstract relationships originally arose as men came to coordinate relations in order to pursue objectives—as game animals were pursued by the original hunting bands. Such bonds were not instinctual or even essentially social but were *contractual alliances*.

The mediated relationship of the contractual agreement may actually encourage gaps to develop in the instinctual social underpinnings. Mediation which is originally a temporary expedient may become the dominant rule. There is the further consideration that leaders can best protect their positions if they disrupt the instinctual solidarity of the men under them. While encouraging impersonalness among the subordinates by switching them around and shuffling them up, they simultaneously implement symbolic and contractual relations among them, over which they, as leaders, are in control. Even in the early Egyptian kingdoms, bureaucrats and scribes were moved around to prevent them from forming an attachment to any one region.

The great structure of America, consisting of an impersonal and radically monotheistic religion and a vastly over-extended bureaucracy, the essence of which is computers and electronic communication systems, can be explained as an attempt to unify an aggregate of randomly assembled individuals who *ab initio* are alien to one another. Indeed, if America were an historically derived and culturally unified people, much less superorganization would be necessary. *Social progress would be unnecessary*.

For example, the great system of courts, the corpus of law and the bureaucracy integrating these principles would be superfluous to the individual. Today, however, what we call crime in America is simply warfare. Wilmot Robertson says: "Both the enemy soldier and, increasingly, the minority lawbreaker feel their crimes are not crimes in the real sense, but simply acts of justifiable violence against an oppressor . . . To most minority prisoners, the modern American prison is little more than a prisoner-of-war camp . . ."[1] While American streets have been compared to jungles—indeed they are more dangerous than any actual jungle—sociologists announce with solemn pomp the "discovery" of some new plan for "rehabilitation." The increment of this pink fog of esoterica, as explained to gullible students and citizens, is the criterion of social progress.

Regarding the economy, a free and competitive system will work successfully only so long as there is an underlying *social* understanding as to the nature and limits of competition, and a strong sense of the point at which economic functions clash with organic social values. The understanding exists in essence only among people of the same race and history, who will co-operate more or less even in the most unregulated economy. In this internal respect, no economy can be without a certain *inward* spirit of socialism. It might be called a socialism of the instincts. This is not a *system* as defined by classical and Marxist economics, but an organic and cultural sensitivity to the interests of the group and the individual alike. If the historical roots of this organic socialism are cut off, even the most coercive system cannot in the long run force men to engage in productive enterprise. Where socialist systems in some sense work, they are rooted in underlying cultures. In America, at the opposite extreme, the regulatory bureaucracy seems to thrive precisely because the competitors do not co-operate in any respect but must be saved from one another. But here it is precisely socialism, which must necessarily intervene, which becomes an argument against pluralism, the *res compositas* of caste specialists.

Thus far, in the face of ethnic diversification, polarization and rising group antagonism, the American supersystem has survived only by re-enforcing its artificially large bureaucracies with electronic systems. The bureaucratic work is done largely by computers which with superhuman speed classify and regiment whole populations. Computers have become virtual symbols of mass regimentation, used as they are as the main tools of "objective study" by sociologists, while for the bureaucrat the "manipulation of data" becomes the manipulation of actual human beings. The spirit of computerized sociology and that of bureaucracy are very close.

Also the mass communications media have been employed to reinforce the supersociety, bridging gaps in the flagging instinctual structure. The media serve not merely to mediate information but to mediate "positive" human relationships. They are in essence a mechanized "contract."

With effusive pleas for harmony and peace pouring from all communications systems, the system must, to prevent the inward restlessness of clashing populations from bursting the seams of society, grow still larger and more rigid and doctrinaire. Meanwhile its internal operation becomes increasingly inefficient, more energy being expended merely in supporting the system irrespective of its special functions.

Society finally comes to live off its own divisions. Its main business is that of pluralism. The individual comes to depend on the divisions of society for his livelihood. In these terms social work and sociology are the makework projects of postwar America just as the Work Projects Administration was the panacea of the Great Depression. If depression is defined as a period where there are not enough *useful* jobs to go around, we are presently in such a depression, one in which men are not given useless menial jobs but useless white-collar jobs. For the creation of every unproductive job (this *is* the contemporary notion of "creativity"), a new job must be invented to integrate it with others.

There are indications that the economy has gone to the end of its possibilities. No longer are people motivated to make bigger and faster cars and airplanes. Sudden economic depressions follow from boredom with existing goods. This technological and material indifference demands a rechanneling of energies into new areas—and the only area left is social projects.

The most ambitious and perhaps even heroic of these tasks, but ultimately a tragically heroic task, is to make the minority citizen into somebody's, the socialist's or the adman's, conception of a Man and a full human being and an equal. This bold mission has become diluted, however, in that it is presently a make-work project for vast numbers of middle-class but unskilled and untalented citizens.

Vast material and human resources must be allocated. "Integration" is expensive, and since it is expensive it "stimulates the economy." It is curious that one argument leveled by sociologists against segregation is that separate facilities, which duplicate restrooms, drinking fountains and restaurants, are inefficient and "a burden to the economy." Citizens' material interests are appealed to in order to overcome what is "morally culpable." However, now that these extra drinking fountains have all been abolished, society is faced with the prospect of supporting —forever and ever—vast armies of sociologists, social workers, civil rights workers and lawyers, investigating services and committees and various and sundry go-betweens and mediators, all of whom, as specially trained men and women, demand to be supported in the style not of welfare recipients but of middle-class citizens.

The WPA led to the creation of some wonderful parks and zoos. All we have to show for our present middle-class make-work project is the numerical increase of minority citizens and the consequent need for more social workers and police. The new middle-class welfare ideas justify themselves by work that is laboriously and dutifully *invented*. The dispenser of welfare and the receiver live off of each other, a contradiction which grows more apparent as the bureaucracy-welfare syndrome becomes a dominant theme of society. It remains to be seen how long a society can feed off itself without consuming some vital organ and killing the system. There is the less obvious principle that mediative and integrative structure, in the sense that it drains spheres of productivity in connecting them, and lives off of what it merely transmits, is a kind of parasitism.

America is a *liberal concept* in that it serves not to build a special and distinctive culture, but the function of bringing together and policing diverse groups and individuals in a single but not very happy household. The cultures and special gifts of these peoples are not accepted as they are but are "adjusted" in order to achieve this integration. Considering art as an example, high art is called by mass democracy "racist" because it affirms the motives and experiences of a particular group. In mass society, therefore, true art is not only difficult but is virtually inverted in the fads of "pop art" and abstractionism. In reconciling disharmonious races it is essential that this very disharmony be somehow contained in the symbols of reconciliation. This inverted art in no sense recognizes its own narrow compulsiveness but regards itself ideologically as esthetic "liberation."

Regarding America's political liberalism, Peter Berger, a sociologist, has correctly seen the paradox of American intellectual and ideological conservatism: "If conservatism has any root meaning, it is that of wanting to preserve the existing order of things. But the existing order of things in America is profoundly liberal, institutionally as well as ideologically. Thus the intellectual conservative in America, deeply critical of liberal ideology as he is, finds himself in the position of standing for the preservation of an order based on all those principles which offend him." [2]

Berger presents a clever paradox which does, indeed,

undermine the intellectual conservatism held widely by men who feel compelled by virtue of some insecurity to abstract what should be a matter of instinct. In posing this paradox, however, Berger gets caught in another one. His own position has long been protected and supported by, and probably could not exist without, his ideological enemy, conservatism. For him the argument is nevertheless really a friendly dialogue which is in a state of status quo equilibrium—a status quo, moreover, supported by the rank and file citizens who are above all resistant to any violent upset. "Contrary to the prophets of doom, there is no indication as yet that this mass of people has changed its basic ideological views." Institutionally speaking, he is right: the bureaucrat and liberal, or any citizens right or left who are so much a part of the institutional structure that they have no identity apart from it, lean on one another. The bureaucrat, a conservative at heart, emphasizes stability and drags his heels. But he is also willing to move so long as it is in an accustomed and predictable direction. And he is most used to having the liberal move him.

Neither the elite nor the intellectual "counter-elite," however, can come up with an appropriate defensive response toward the movements of anti-structure breaking out in all sectors of society: populism among the farmers and factory workers, hippy-ism and a new religiosity among the youth and, finally, a bitter frustration and willingness to "let things take care of themselves" within the middle class. The paradox of the liberal-conservative status quo is that the bureaucratic and legal structure which the dialogue takes for granted has as its energy source the existential population, from which, however, by discoursing only within its own system, the structure alienates itself.

A contradiction invariably develops in the process of superorganization. True creativity has its source in an instinctual cohesiveness and tribalism. This energy is necessary not only in tasks of culture but in building abstract bureaucracies and exchange systems. However, the tribal and racial group which, in attempting to draw remote groups into its systems, even when this effort has a purely selfish objective, must finally subject itself to its own abstract coercion; the group finally atomizes itself. The system-builders thereby cut themselves off from their creative source and original purpose.

XI

THE REVERSAL OF WORLD HISTORY

All life—and human life is not an exception—is *segmented*. In each living body there are halves which are essentially obverse sides of the same unity. Primitive societies have moieties, dividing themselves into opposing segments. Each segment has its mythological and ritual symbols which express a unity of opposition within the society. There is often much bickering on a personal level, which is reversed by rituals of harmony and reconciliation on a symbolic level. When a group breaks up, its line of fission corresponds to the moiety lines, much like the process of cell mitosis.

In becoming organized, however, living beings do not overcome the fact of segmentation. On the contrary, complex societies define this opposition more sharply and emphatically. To overcome the elemental dialectic of nature through the absolute universal abstraction of a "world society" would be to finally and absolutely negate the fundamental fact of biology and instinct. Human life, out of blind will to survive, backs away from such a possibility.

Total organization of life on earth was achieved immediately following World War II in the opposition of Eastern and Western blocs. Finally, having absorbed all other national feelings and viewpoints, the ideologies of East and West, the communist and democratic-pluralistic ideologies, confronted one another in an absolute and final opposition. And yet they were two sides of the *same* universality, opposites which could not be transcended. The international mediator, in trying to synthesize these adversaries with an absolute abstraction, hit with fatal finality upon the raw urgency of instincts. The real barrier to an absolute monolithic world economy and society was not, however, ideology. It was rather a basic organic and psychological barrier.

As the absolute world state approached, the means, both physical and psychological, for preventing such a society grew in direct proportion. Movement towards world government, a trend made possible by communications, transportation and computer technology, was accompanied by the development of an *absolute barrier* which was also technological—the atom weapon. Whether war is actually more terrible now than it ever was is not the question. Europeans once spread germs wholesale to Indians in a kind of biological warfare, while still earlier entire populations were decimated by an instrument no more sophisticated than the sword. The primary consideration is simply that people think of the atom bomb as the ultimate weapon. This fear of war to the point where it is thought impossible derives from the fact that no greater social synthesis of nations can be accomplished.

However, it will still be some time before this fundamental intuition expresses itself within formal institutions, in which universalism is inherent as the Hegelian "idea." Institutions *as such*, as abstractions, are out of step or even at odds with world history in that their "idea" is mediation. History today aims at particularity and individuality, the immediacy that is the essence of culture. For that reason, life will ultimately overwhelm "progressive" institutions and replace them with direct and intuitive human relationships. Life will revive the private and personal bond which the supersociety has so drastically subverted.

The wave of the future is regionalism, a continuity of formed, disciplined instincts. The world order Roderick

Seidenberg prophesized is already in the past: "The organization of society will unquestionably proceed until its final crystallization shall have been achieved ecumenically, because of the relationship of this trend with the inherent dominance of the principle of intelligence." [1] This "icy grandeur," as Seidenberg describes it, does not appear to describe the recent trends of history.

The accomplishment of regionalism will be through the level-by-level internalization of violence. This internal fighting will obviously begin in the super-blocs. Since they cannot fight between themselves—it is overwhelmingly believed that war on their scale of technology would annihilate all life—their component nations will assert themselves in compulsive struggles of "liberation." Turning away from the absolute barrier dividing the final world-segments ultimately means an increase of local violence, which in isolated cases can be seen breaking out even now.

XII

THE REVOLT AGAINST MEDIATION

The closer history moved toward an absolute world society, and the more integrative institutions gained priority over the concrete elements of culture, the higher the mediator rose in these structures—which were essentially extensions of the mediator himself. Also, the population of mediators grew more numerous.

Even though history and "social progress" is conspicuously reversing itself, the American institutional viewpoint continues to regard institutions as breaking away from regional and racial societies and toward an absolute world synthesis. Abstract structures are programmed to expunge and expel from themselves qualities associated with particular peoples and regions. This is the so-called silent and bloodless revolution of which communications, religious and teaching establishments proudly speak. They now openly ask: "After the Revolution—now what?!"

It is not accurate to describe this revolution as liberal or conservative, but as professionalist. Professionalism is defined here as the institutional viewpoint regarding the tasks and destiny of institutions. Professionalism may be seen positively as a commitment to one's work. But it is also a total viewpoint, one by virtue of which a man suffers uprootedness and deracination along with the structures with which he identifies. In short, the professionalist is a machine, an automaton who desires to free himself from all "entangling" influences from lay pressure and from commitments to realities outside his specific sphere of functioning. This is the case not only in communications media and other "liberal" institutions but in all operations subject to professionalism, in any area of activity from the manufacture of breakfast foods to athletics, which are increasingly insistent on autonomy in setting policies and standards.

Since the "idea" of institutions is mediation, it can be understood why, as they liberate themselves from regional and racial roots, they become increasingly antagonistic to regional culture, which is organically self-contained and closed. A culture, as formed life, draws around itself a horizon which sets it apart from other life. The definition of culture is a *sublimated* form which is inextricably entangled and "corrupted" by its appropriate content, its sensuous historical experience, its racial constitution.

The values of America as the halfway abstraction of Europe-in-general were simply sentimental and prosaic. The absolute mediating institutions identify with values antithetical to any regionality. In systems built up around the outside personality of the mediator, values are inverted. Today the mass media conspicuously and even militantly tend to idealize ugly, corrosive and demoralizing images and values. Bourgeois sentimentality and patriotism have been turned around as a gleeful nihilism and raised as such to a solemn ethical mission. Pornography is democratic sex which replaces private and exclusive and exclusivist, in other words, "racist" eroticism. Indolence is the obverse media-ized image of the bourgeois values of work. Universalism means anti-nationalism and anti-WASPism, the WASP being the hypothetical "native." The ethnic is the ideal American in that he is construed as a non-American.

The abstract image of life is a mirror image, that is, a *reversed* image where everything is backward. This is not to say, however, that institutions do not at least theoretically affirm a relationship to actual, viable and instinctual life. They fear that any real enthusiasm or anger will topple them. But institutions can deal with life only by abstracting it. Abstracted life, however, is a contradiction in terms. Abstraction is generalization about what by nature is particular and individual. This inversion has the ultimate practical consequence that institutions not only cannot predict life, but predict the opposite of what actually transpires. Built into institutions is the view of their own progress—thus "social progress." In every case where mediative structures of "reconciliation" have pronounced such predictions, the world has been rapidly on the way to strife and war. There is a simple reason for this. As structures rise above particular men, the *men* become as autonomous as the institutions; and their instincts tell them to pursue egoistic aims. This individualism and deteriorating empathy in turn require extra democratic "optimism."

The most overtly, externally and trivially alive person is the stereotype Negro. The black man is viewed as the greatest threat and the one who must be appeased and brought into the system. The white man, then, considering himself entirely institutionalized and in this sense domesticated, logically excludes the fact that *he* could be a threat to his own structures. In reducing his activity to systems he buries and obscures his life energy; he forgets it is there. But as C. G. Jung has observed, autonomous libido is explosive and dangerous.

The sterotype black man has himself become an American institution, not so much unto himself (although he sees himself in white institutional terms as a ferocious guerrilla fighter). Rather he is an institution to white people. His mere existence in the center of the American cities is to be attributed to institutions because, rightly or wrongly, whites privately tend to consider him mostly useless. Although he may live on welfare in squalid ghettos, he has become a living symbol of pluralistic democracy. This pluralism began as that of the Anglo-Saxons versus Irish and Germans, but it evolved into the pluralism of black and white. The Negro, then, is the one for whom democratic rights seem specially created. He is the basic reason for existence of both the mediation establishment and of America's leading institutions. Paradoxically, universities are turning out a class of people—sociologists, poverty workers and civil rights lawyers—who live off the Negro! Society must not only support him, it must support his nurses and babysitters. Black people themselves have nothing to say about this, since civil rights is welfare for a great and powerful white interest group.

The black man's so-called African qualities, or a fiction of them, are not suppressed but, on the contrary, are brought out. Even the most morally involved anthropologist must smile at the pseudo-Africanisms which could just as well have been the invention of admen as of the black man himself. The fact is that these Afro-American styles and mannerisms are inversions of real or imagined WASP traits. As an inverted citizen the mediators need the Negro as much as he needs them. The emerging ideal of American democracy is an abstract priesthood governing an amorphous colored mass. The black man's new success is reflected not in a high individual living standard but, appropriate to his status as the democratic man, in a conspicuous, luxurious, opulent and utterly unrestricted rate of reproduction.

It is a mistake of the black man to think he is fighting institutions when in fact he is the content of them, or that his enemy is the policeman who actually protects him from the ominous anarchist violence of the whites! A grave mistake! However, the black man will probably survive his mistake if only because he is not an institution unto himself but unto white people. The full impact of the revolt of life and instincts—we could call it white power—which before the deterioration of the world society was buried and latent, will fall rather upon the hyper-institutionalized man himself. This person, regardless of ethnic or racial affiliation, is so permeated with the abstractness of the structures with which he identifies that he must fall with them.

XIII

THE FALL OF THE MEDIATOR

Anarchism is the impulse to tear down society. But few anarchists want to abolish society altogether. They want only to tear it down to a certain point. It is in terms of what they want to keep that it is possible to distinguish left-wing from right-wing anarchists. Leftists would like to break down society and culture until only an *idea* remains. Rightists would keep only the elemental fact of *race*.

The idea which for the left takes the place of race is the idea of "universal humanity." The left presently *is* humanity. It is outsiders lacking internal cohesion but having relationships through the abstraction of "mankind." The obvious example of an intellectual establishment of this kind was the Sophists, who came together from various distant regions throughout the Mediterranean and Near East. In Greece they formed themselves as an association of teachers of logic and rhetoric. Their mental gymnastics and witty tricks with logic made them exceedingly popular, and they drew large crowds wherever they went. However, they were casually and without much anxiety regarded as vaguely subversive. They were not friendly to Greek culture and could be accused of impiety regarding its gods. As an alternative to existing society, they advocated an early form of social engineering in which all society would be reduced to the *terms of logic*—the same logic they taught as a pure science.

The condition of being minorities and outsiders once characterized all Americans. America was not one region among others but was settled as the halfway abstraction of Europe-in-general, a concept which is the premise of American pluralistic democracy. Democratic ideology has served the positive function of softening cultural distinctions. There is now beginning to emerge an inward feeling for a new American population comprised of Europeans who have marginally hybridized racially and culturally. This new race would still retain great diversity; the American ethnic groups, insofar as they are presently identifiable, would retain a certain identity, perhaps in different regions of America. Once Americans are again secure in their personal relationships and feel a sense of regional permanence, it may be expected that religion and art will undergo a new efflorescence. Society will *break down*, rather than build up, to the optimum community size for art.

But this new biological and cultural unity is scarcely what is envisioned in the ideological structure of democratic institutions, which allow only the abstract expression of tribal culture as most perfectly embodied in the absolute "outside" cultures, say, of the Indian and Negro. The intuitive and institutionally inexpressible feeling for a new American population is the basis of the recently insurgent regionalism, which is presently causing bewildering defections from the Democratic and Republican political camps.

The ideologies of the right and left both attack "existing institutions," but the left urges men to push on to the "end" of culture—a world *civitas maxima*, an absolute abstraction. Existing American institutions are indeed still programmed to continue in this direction, on the assumption that the world society lies in the future. Their Hegelian "ideas" still strive to free themselves from particular concrete cultural and regional contents, in order to extend themselves universally. It is increasingly apparent, however, that the world society has already come and gone.

Moving in the opposite direction, populism urges us to recapture the beginnings of culture in elemental realities of race, region and basic values.

The new populism is not ideological conservatism. In the first place, fiscal conservatism lost its fight when it failed to distinguish capital as money committed to a specific culture from, on the other hand, money which is a disembodied abstract power by its own right. Capitalism as a particular and historical growth has been confused with the free enterprise *system*. Conservatism also could have saved religion, which is the compromised regional social conscience of national capitalism. Pure money, however, demanded a much more rigid and abstract ideological social conscience. Absolute money necessitated the ideology of mankind, which, far from contradicting the idea of God, was the essence of this idea—God as the mediating father of mankind who was interposed in relationships universally. So-called conservatism has played into the hands of liberalism on every meaningful issue by starting from the same premise, namely, that social relationships are in essence *contractual*. On this point American conservatives have perhaps been most influenced by Ortega y Gasset. The spiritual fathers of the new conservative populism, however, are Spengler and Dostoyevsky.

American culture from the beginning, as the halfway abstraction of Europe-in-general, was not a regional extension of a continuity growing out of the parent continent but the abstraction of the superregion as a whole transplanted to new soil. It is not surprising, then, that Ortega, the advocate of a European superstate, should be the philosopher capable of evoking enthusiasm from all ideological factions. Finally, however, American democracy as a mediating ideal attempted, in a sequence of self-negation, to express this ideal as a democracy of Man-in-general. America, where races came together from the far corners of the earth, became the nation of mankind.

This is to say Americans pulled their halfway abstraction in two ways: (1) toward an absolute universal abstraction, humanity, which would include not only regional Americans but the most particular of all men, the Negro, and the most universal of all men, the mediator; (2) in the other direction toward an absolutely concrete unity of land and people which would not be "generally European" but one more regional culture growing out of Europe. America would indeed be fully American when it divided further into a plurality of cultures and regions. To actually encourage this regionalism and separatism, and thus *now* be in step with historical inevitability, is the aspiration of regionalism.

Middle-Americans, the bourgeoisie that considered itself most American, have disappointed the world, particularly after brilliant beginnings. They are now incapable of any greater contribution to the arts than magazine illustrations, soap operas and ice shows, where culture finally sold out to the abstract ideology of internationalism. In the face of little opposition, America decided for the universalist abstraction. On the physical level, culture dissolved into the absolute space of communications and transportation technology. In its ecumenical "revelling in empty dimension," as Spengler put it, America was not only consistent with the overall trend of world history but it led that history. As a society of raceless humanity, America provided the *idea* of humanity for half the world. America was largely a land of alienated minorities which, for that reason, followed the leadership of the Jews as the most successful mediators in past times. The other "international" idea was provided by Russia, itself a welter of minorities asserting themselves through mediation of Marxism. These great ecumenical ideas, however, instead of containing a plan for their own synthesis, clashed head on and without compromise. This is not to say that world organization was defeated. It is simply that no unity rooted to any extent in organic realities can transcend the elemental fact of segmentation. But even this "segmented" unity is now breaking apart.

This organic reversal does not mean, however, that institutions are reorienting themselves accordingly. Institutions are always behind the times. The uncertainty and disorientation in America today is that its hierarchies and ideologies are still programmed in anticipation of a *civitas maxima*, which in fact is already in the past.

The anarchism of the left proved to be the distruction of what I called the "halfway" abstraction of Europe-in-general to make way for the absolute abstraction of humanity, the world society. What is overlooked is that this inevitable historical process, which made the left victorious, stopped with *two* societies whose internal orientation derived from opposition to one another. The left has expected the segments to be finally transcended in an ultimate act of super-mediation, each idea yielding to the ultimate universalism which was implicit in both of them. Instead, however, the ideologies have lately sold out by degrees to regionalism. For all their internal social engineering, Russia and China have become nationalist in relation to one another. Marxism has become Leninism and Maoism. The United States, which could never gain total dominion over Africa and South America, was confronted by the Third World. In Peru communism has had to make an embarrassing alliance with a strange "Inca nationalism." Appearing everywhere are regionalist struggles of "liberation." Only for purposes of world sanction and immediate material support do these revolts identify themselves as communist or democratic. In reality they are populist, or essentially non-ideological.

Lately the word populism has been dug out of a dusty closet of American history to describe a new mixture of leftist and rightist radicalism. Originally populism appeared in the Middle West as a farmer's protest against dominance by railroads and banks. But today populism is fast rising in urban areas. There is the same affirmation of basic values against abstract organizational principles. The South, which has always been populist, has come forth with vigorous political leaders to hold a strange sway over urban masses. The word populist seems to exert a mysterious power. It sticks. Meanwhile journalists and professors and mediative bureaucrats attempted to enlist the term for their own tired purposes. They nervously suggest a "new populist coalition" of the poor and oppressed of all races, a conception patently related to the hopelessly theoretical "proletariat." A populist coalition is a contradiction in terms since populism in essence is not any kind of "alliance" but an inward unity of men of like culture and race. The new populism, as before, is hostile to the abstractions of bureaucracy and money, as well as to the bluff of establishment intellectuals. Big money is the thief of farmlands and the distorter of basic values. But the populist is equally intolerant of forced and unnatural interpersonal relationships. "Integration," the *ignis fatuus* of the mediator, is abhorrent not so much because the black man is abhorrent but because forced contact requires, as a dimension of mediation, an abstract buffer which depersonalizes and demoralizes relationships. The "soil" of the new populism is not only the land but, for the urban working man, the elemental tribal and ethnic and racial population.

XIV
CONCLUSION

The power and fame of the mediator depend on the fact that there are divisions in society. These are more than boundaries defining economic specialization and social avoidance; they are real and volatile antagonisms. The trick of being a go-between consists, then, not simply of bringing men together or reconciling them, but of reconciling them through the special symbols of mediation. On the other hand, this level of abstract integration can be accomplished only by pitting men against one another and keeping them estranged on a personal and instinctual level. But they cannot be made to reject one another so thoroughly that they reject the whole idea of mediation. Nor can they be brought together in such a way that they fuse organically, in which case they would also lose interest in mediation.

The question remains, do people wish to sacrifice organic cohesion for impersonal systemization? The *res communitas* and *res compositas* come into direct antagonism when the mediator tries to "open" the former to the latter. This means disturbing internal values. The regional society may be affirmative regarding the mediator insofar as it wants outside relationships while maintaining its internal cultural discreteness. On the other hand, the mediator can assist what he regards as his mission by subjecting regional values to rational-abstract criticism, rationality being also the basis of "outside" values from which derive, ultimately, abstract money and ideology as the "social conscience" of money. Consequently the aim of the mediator is not to remain an outsider between groups of insiders, but to make all men outsiders, who are incapable of relationships other than those maintained through the mediating symbols. However, this interference is a dangerous business.

It is not likely that the American liberal actually wants total racial miscegenation. Rather he wants "integration" wherein men turn away from one another altogether and toward the priests of civil rights. The purpose of bringing the races together in intimate contact and in space originally relegated for social purposes is not to force them together on the level of instinctual society but, on the contrary, to make any such society impossible.

As uprooted Europeans who were already partially estranged and more interested in economics than in social relationships, Americans are highly dependent on the mediator. America has become a civilization of mediation and the mediator. But even here his strategy is being thwarted. The various white nationalities are marginally closing together and developing a sense of common culture and race. The go-betweens are in haste to disrupt this understanding before it closes them out altogether. For his part, however, the black man, although violently expressing resentment of his past treatment, shows ever greater reluctance to co-operate in any plan of integration. He is increasingly separating himself not only socially but institutionally and symbolically, at first within the very systems which had accepted him through "integration" but more recently in increasingly remote and insular groupings and cults. Physically speaking, the cities which had once absorbed him are shifting their spatial focus away from the so-called inner city, thus eventually isolating him outside.

These separatist tendencies spell eventual disaster for the mediation establishment, if not for the whole principle of democratic pluralism. Robertson says: "[If] Negro separatism should ever become the order of the day, other unassimilable minorities might take the hint, leaving liberalism an ideology in search of a party. At the other extreme, total integration would deal an equally lethal blow to the liberal-minority axis by spelling the doom of all minorities and with them liberalism's *raison d'être*. It is only in the boundary zone between the segregated and the integrated society, between reality and utopia, that the modern liberal feels at home." [1]

The go-between spans between factions and peoples. His power and prosperity are based on the fact that the groups depend upon one another and yet cannot have relationships except through him. However, the paradox of his situation is that any contact which compromises internal cultural values—and most contact with outsiders is felt to compromise them to some degree—is "betrayal." It makes no sense to call the mediator a traitor since expressions of loyalty to a country or people must, in his case, be coerced. But from the viewpoint of discrete peoples, the reconciler, the man whose only desire is for international and interracial peace and co-operation, is in his deepest nature "disloyal." While he could not be a mediator if he owed allegiance to any nation or people, even perhaps his own abstract "nation" of mediators, he puts himself in a delicate position. He is inevitably identified with the interests of the opposing party, hence he is regarded as against the in-group. From the standpoint of the in-group, mediation always has a poisonous element. It is utterly imperative, if the mediator is to survive in this climate of hostility, that the groups continue to need contact; and that they nevertheless remain separate and even hostile so as to require his services. The go-between must be clever indeed to preserve this fragile balance in the unpredictable chaos of world politics.

Notes

CHAPTER I

1. Max Stirner, *Der Einzige und sein Eigentum und andere Schriften*, ed. H. G. Helms, Carl Hanser Verlag, Munich, 1968, p. 153. My translation.
2. H. G. Wells, *Outline of History*, Garden City Publishing Company, Garden City, New York, 1929, p. 597.
3. Arnold J. Toynbee, *A Study of History*, ed. D. C. Somerville, Oxford University Press, N.Y., 1947, p. 175.
4. Amrit Lal, "Ethnic Minorities of Mainland China," *Mankind Quarterly*, Vol. VIII, No. 4.
5. Jean-Jacques Rousseau, *The Social Contract*, trans. Willmoore Kendall, Henry Regnery Company, Chicago, 1971, p. 3.
6. José Ortega y Gasset, *The Revolt of the Masses*, trans. anonymous, W. W. Norton and Company, New York, 1957, p. 170.

CHAPTER II

1. Otto Gierke, *Natural Law and the Theory of Society: 1500–1800*, Beacon Press, Boston, 1957, p. 115.
2. *Ibid.*, p. 166.
3. Claude Lévi-Strauss, "The Scope of Anthropology," *Current Anthropology*, Vol. 7, No. 2, p. 115. Cf. also Hugo G. Nutini, "The Ideological Basis of Lévi-Strauss' Structuralism," read at the Convention of the American Anthropological Association, 11/23/69, mimeographed, pp. 15–17.
4. Wells, *Outline*, pp. 531–32.

CHAPTER IV

1. Otto Friedrich Bollnow, *Mensch und Raum*, W. Kohlhammer Verlag, Stuttgart, 1963, p. 80. My translation.
2. Ortega y Gasset, *Revolt*, p. 172.

CHAPTER V

1. Karl Marx, *Capital*, Encyclopaedia Britannica, Inc., Chicago, p. 40.
2. Oswald Spengler, "Der Streitwagen und seine Bedeutung für den Gang der Weltgeschichte," *Reden und Aufsätze*, C. H. Beck'sche Verlagsbuchhandlung, Munich, 1951, p. 150. My translation.
3. Wells, *Outline*, p. 134.
4. *Ibid.*, p. 218.
5. C. D. Darlington, *The Evolution of Man and Society*, George Allen and Unwin, London, 1969, p. 177.
6. W. Lloyd Warner, *Yankee City*, Yale University Press, New Haven, 1963.
7. Stirner, *Der Einzige*, p. 88.
8. Oswald Spengler, *Jahre der Entscheidung*, Deutscher Taschenbuch Verlag, Munich, 1961, p. 107.
9. Wilmot Robertson, *The Dispossessed Majority*, Howard Allen, Box 76, Cape Canaveral, Florida, 1972, p. 231.

CHAPTER VI

1. Victor Turner, *The Ritual Process: Structure and Anti-Structure*, Aldine Publishing Company, 1969, p. 14. Cf. also Turner's statement: "[Among] the Ndembu there is a close connection between social conflict and ritual at the levels of village and . . . discrete clusters of villages, and . . . a multiplicity of conflict situations is correlated with a high frequency of ritual performance." p. 10.
2. Wells, *Outline*, p. 190.
3. Darlington, *The Evolution*, pp. 102–03.
4. Wells, *Outline*, p. 352.
5. Alfonso Caso, *The Aztecs: People of the Sun*, University of Oklahoma Press, Norman, Oklahoma, 1958.
6. *Ibid.*, p. 519.
7. *Ibid.*, p. 531–32.
8. Darlington, *The Evolution*, p. 208.
9. Spengler, *Jahre*, p. 127.
10. Wells, *Outline*, p. 539.

CHAPTER VII

1. Ernst Haeckel, *The Riddle of the Universe*, Harper and Brothers, New York, 1902, p. 206.
2. Stirner, *Der Einzige*, p. 118.

CHAPTER VIII

1. Wells, *Outline*, p. 232.

CHAPTER X

1. Robertson, *Dispossessed*, p. 425.
2. Peter L. Berger, "Two Paradoxes," *National Review*, May 12, 1972, p. 508.

CHAPTER XI

1. Roderick Seidenberg, *Posthistoric Man*, Beacon Press, Boston, 1957, p. 179.

CHAPTER XIV

1. Robertson, *Dispossessed*, p. 221.

Index